The Fruit of the Spirit

Alan Cairns

AMBASSADOR
EMERALD INTERNATIONAL

Greenville, South Carolina • Belfast, Northern Ireland
www.emeraldhouse.com

The Fruit of the Spirit

Scripture refrences are from the King James Version.

Ambassador Emerald International
427 Wade Hampton Boulevard
Greenville, S.C. 29609 U.S.A.

and

Ambassador Productions Ltd.
Providence House
Ardenlee Street
Belfast BT6 8QJ, Northern Ireland

www.emeraldhouse.com

Cover design and page layout by A & E Media, Sam Laterza

ISBN 1 889893 91 9

Contents

Acknowledgments

Two ladies were of particular help in preparing the material of this book for publication. First, amid many other responsibilities my wife, Joan, did all the initial typing. Then Judy Brown edited and proofread the whole work. Judy's schedule is always full and I deeply appreciate her willingness to take on the added burden of this work. To Joan and Judy, then, I express my thanks. Without them this book would not now be in your hands.

I must acknowledge the goodness of God in His blessing on these studies when they were preached. It pleased Him to use them in the lives of many of His people in three widely separated congregations: first, in my own congregation in Greenville, South Carolina; then in the Free Presbyterian Church, Newtownards, Northern Ireland (at least they heard a few of them, for I lost my voice early in the week of special meetings!); and finally in Faith Bible Church, Pearl City, Hawaii. The response in all three places was an encouragement to make the studies available to a wider public in printed form. I thank each of these congregations for their expressions of support and trust that they will be blessed again as they read *The Fruit of the Spirit*.

To

Nevin Carson,

a ruling elder in

Ballymoney Free Presbyterian Church,

Northern Ireland,

who is now with Christ,

and to his wife, Marjorie,

I gratefully dedicate this book.

All who have worked with them have found

in their lives much of the fruit of the Spirit.

Spiritual Fighting and Fruitbearing

Galatians 5:16–23

Foolish men sometimes say wise things. Charles Caleb Colton was an unsavory Church of England clergyman who was addicted to gambling and who died a suicide. Yet he produced *Lacon, or many things in a few words addressed to those who think*, a two-volume "collection of aphorisms of an edifying kind, and very often forcibly expressed" (*National Dictionary of Biography*). One of Colton's penetrating statements was probably a summary of his own life: "Man is an embodied paradox, a bundle of contradictions" (*Lacon*, 1.408).

"A bundle of contradictions" is indeed an apt description of man! We see this bundle of contradictions in the lives of even the best of men, for the best of men at best are only men. On Mount Carmel, Elijah stood like a Colossus against all the furious hatred and frenzy of hundreds of the prophets of Baal and dared the king of Israel's wrath. However, almost immediately after having routed his enemies he fled when he received a venomous letter from Jezebel. Peter was an intrepid warrior who stood for the Lord Jesus Christ against the armed thugs who came after Him in Gethsemane. Yet a few hours later, under the shrill questioning of a slip of a girl, he denied that he even knew the Saviour. Paul rejoiced in Christian victory and abundant life, but yet confessed, "The things that I do I allow [approve] not" and referred to his body as a "body of death."

We must all confess that we are bundles of contradictions. We find Paul's experience mirrored in our own lives. Conflicting forces are at work in every Christian. His life is a battleground, and even though he gains the victory, he laments many setbacks. Paul spoke to the Galatians about these conflicting forces. He spoke of them as "the flesh" and "the Spirit": "This I say then, Walk in the Spirit, and ye shall not fulfil the lust of the flesh. For the flesh lusteth against the Spirit, and the Spirit against the flesh: and these are contrary the one to the other: so that ye cannot do the things that ye would" (Galatians 5:16–17).

God has called His people to liberty: "Brethren, ye have been called unto liberty; only use not liberty for an occasion to the flesh" (Galatians 5:13). But Christian liberty is not a license to sin. As the Bible commentator Albert Barnes remarked, "It is not freedom from virtuous restraints and from the laws of God. It is liberty from the servitude of sin, and religious rites and ceremonies, not freedom from the necessary restraints of virtue. . . . Paul is . . . at great pains to show that the doctrine which he had maintained did not lead to licentiousness, and did not allow the indulgence of sinful and corrupt passions." Paul shows us that the Holy Spirit conducts an unremitting warfare against the flesh to subdue its characteristic operations, and at the same time He produces the fruit of grace in the lives of God's people.

Thus we must commence our study of life in the Spirit by spending a little time on the subject of spiritual fighting and fruitbearing.

The Flesh

We must note, first of all, that the flesh is an active, evil power that constantly seeks to assert itself in God's people. "The flesh lusteth against the Spirit, and the Spirit against the flesh: and these are contrary the one to the other: so that ye cannot do the things that ye would" (Galatians 5:17). The flesh is "the old man" (the old Adam) in us that is always discernible by its desire—or, *lust,* to use Paul's expression—to have self in control. The flesh opposes the Spirit of God, who indwells every believer in Christ. It opposes all things spiritual and proposes what is carnal and pleasing to self. It dims our view of eternity and focuses our attention on the things of time.

We need to be aware of the flesh's constant attempt to assert itself, and we must understand the radical deduction that Paul draws from that fact. Because of the ceaseless warfare between the flesh and the Spirit, the apostle says, "These are contrary the one to the other: so that ye cannot do the things that ye would." The word *cannot* may be rendered "should not." What this Scripture says, therefore, is that in view of the flesh's constant attempts to assert itself in us we should not do anything simply because we have a desire to do it. "I want to do this," or "I feel like doing this," is never a good enough reason for a Christian to act. We must never define what is right by what we desire or by how we feel. When we feel a desire to do something, we need to examine our hearts to discover whether the desire in question is a product of the flesh or of the Spirit—a matter that must be settled by the objective standard of the word of God, not by the feelings of our flesh. This is what counts. Our flesh is corrupt and deceitful. It wages an unending war against everything spiritual and godly within us. That is a fact of life and we do well never to forget it.

The Fight

We must note a second truth from our text: The Holy Spirit evidences His presence in a believer by opposing the dominion of his flesh and subduing its operations. Sin no longer reigns in a believer in Christ. It is no longer the sole possessor of his heart. Indeed, now it is an intruder and a usurper whose activity is a grief to his soul.

This is a vital evidence of the presence of the Holy Spirit in a person. The Spirit causes such a revulsion against sin that when a believer succumbs to the flesh he does not approve of his own action. Rather, he delights in the law of God after the inward man (see Romans 7:15, 22). Though he falls, a believer no longer lives in habitual bondage to the gross passions of the flesh. Paul listed some of these gross passions—"adultery, fornication, uncleanness, lasciviousness, idolatry, witchcraft, hatred, variance, emulations, wrath, strife, seditions, heresies, envyings, murders, drunkenness, revellings, and such like"—and said, "They which do such things shall not inherit the kingdom of God" (Galatians 5:19–21). In other words, people who are ruled by such things are still not saved. Though a believer has to struggle with the motions of his flesh urging him to sin, he is now "led by the Spirit" (Galatians 5:18), who always fights against the flesh and its lusts.

The Holy Spirit never leads a man to indulge the lusts of the flesh. When a believer feels inclined to any action that is contrary to the expressed will of God in the Scripture or that he knows to be the product of his own "old man," he must not delude himself that the Holy Spirit is leading him to take that action. For example, sometimes a Christian

3

with an unsaved spouse who is faithful to the marriage union but unsympathetic to anything spiritual, has been tempted to think something like this: "I feel God intended us all to have happy, united, Christian homes. My spouse is not a Christian and shows no interest in the things of God. Thus we have little in common. I have met someone in church, however, with whom I could be very happy and who would be a spiritual help to me. We feel very much drawn to each other. Surely it cannot be wrong for me to leave my ungodly spouse and to seek a happy Christian home with a believing partner." Once a person gets involved in this kind of self-pitying thought he is on a slippery path to terrible sin and failure. In any such situation the first question to be faced is, Has God's word made any statement about this matter? It has. And it leaves no doubt that a Christian's duty is to maintain the marriage bond (Matthew 19:9; 1 Corinthians 7:12–16).

Many other examples of the specious thinking with which the flesh seeks to corrupt the obedience of Christians may be given, but one more will suffice. An employer is mean and defrauds an employee of his rightful remuneration and that employee thinks, "This man owes me money but won't willingly give it to me. I feel that I have a right to what is mine, so if he won't give it to me I will take it for myself." And so he pilfers from the coffers of his employer's business. But however much he believes that his employer owes him a better wage, he has God's command not to steal. His employer's meanness does not exonerate him from the guilt of theft, and all the self-justifying argument in the world cannot hide the fact that it is his own sinful flesh that leads him to steal, not the Spirit of God. The Spirit always opposes and subdues the motions of the flesh.

From all this we may conclude a very important practical truth: When a Christian feels himself pulled in doubtful directions and has a conflict in his conscience, he should recognize that the deep unease he feels is the work of the Holy Spirit. Unless we can act with a clear conscience in the full light of the word of God, we will probably act carnally and not under the guidance of the Holy Spirit. Thus Paul commands us, "Grieve not the Spirit" (Ephesians 4:30) and "Quench not the Spirit" (1 Thessalonians 5:19). These are commands not to disobey what we know to be the mind of the Spirit because He has made it plain in Scripture, and not to ignore the promptings of the Spirit in our conscience in all matters about which we entertain some doubt or uncertainty. Rather, we should "walk in the Spirit," for this is the one sure way that we will "not fulfil the lust of the flesh" (Galatians 5:16).

The Fruit

Having dealt with the reality of spiritual fighting against the flesh we must consider the other reality that Paul emphasizes in our text: The Holy Spirit does more than oppose the works of the flesh; He also produces spiritual fruit as the governing virtues of a believer's life. "The fruit of the Spirit is love, joy, peace, longsuffering, gentleness, goodness, faith, meekness, temperance: against such there is no law" (Galatians 5:22–23).

The proof of spiritual life is spiritual fruit. If God has planted the root of saving grace in a man, it will produce the fruit of godliness. It is important to note that we are speaking of *fruit,* not works that may be produced by fleshly effort. Andrew Murray points out the difference: "Have you ever noticed the difference in the Christian life between work and fruit? A machine can do work; only life can bear fruit." The fruit of the Spirit is the product of the life He has imparted to the believer. It is the natural expression of the new man in Christ. Jesus said, "Abide in me, and I in you. As the branch cannot bear fruit of itself, except it abide in the vine; no more can ye, except ye abide in me. I am the vine, ye are the branches: he that abideth in me, and I in him, the same bringeth forth much fruit: for without me ye can do nothing" (John 15:4–5).

This spiritual fruit grows in every area of a believer's life. Paul gives us a nine-fold description of the fruit of the Spirit, nine aspects of that fruit that together describe the normal Christian life. These nine specific virtues fall into three groups of three. The first three—love, joy, peace— describe the fruit Christians bear in relation to God. The second three— longsuffering, gentleness, goodness—describe the fruit we bear in relation to others. The third three—faith, meekness, temperance—describe the fruit we bear in relation to ourselves. So spiritual fruitbearing has an upward aspect, an outward aspect, and an inward aspect.

This fruit fulfils the law of God, but does not bring us under legal bondage. Paul makes two significant statements that establish this truth. In Galatians 5:18 he says, "If ye be led of the Spirit, ye are not under the law." Then after listing the nine aspects of the fruit of the Spirit he adds, "Against such there is no law" (verse 23). The apostle's point is that while spiritual fruit in a Christian's life will honor the law of God, it cannot be produced by the works of the law. It is the product of a living union with Christ, the result of a living faith.

Thus Paul commands us, "Walk in the Spirit." That is, live in the Spirit. Follow His leading as He instructs our conscience through His word. As we do so He will conquer the otherwise ungovernable passions of the old man and will produce spiritual fruit to enable us to live right in relation to God, to others, and to ourselves.

Spiritual Fruit— What It Is and How It Is Produced

"The fruit of the Spirit is love, joy, peace, longsuffering, gentleness, goodness, faith, meekness, temperance: against such there is no law."
Galatians 5:22–23

Here is what Christian living is meant to be. The nine-fold fruit of the Spirit describes the essence of true Christian character, the character of a person who is living life to the full on all fronts. This is the potential that lies in every believer in Christ. While no Christian on earth is sinlessly perfect, each one is in the process of realizing this potential. To some degree every believer experiences the Holy Spirit producing this fruit in him. It comes with being a Christian.

As we have already seen, the Christian life is one of spiritual fighting and fruitbearing. We must wage a constant warfare against the old man, the flesh that never ceases to lust against the Spirit. But the Spirit of God indwells us so that we have the authority and the ability to overcome the flesh. Whereas we were once condemned by our unregenerate nature to fulfil the lusts of the flesh, now as God's new creation in Christ we have a new king on the throne of our heart, governing our understanding and will. Thus we are free to bring forth the fruit of the Spirit.

But what is this fruit of the Spirit and how is it produced?

Fruit, Not Duties

We must emphasize that it is fruit that Paul speaks about, not duties. He is not describing the steps by which we become new creatures, but the result of our having been made new creatures. Thus he gives no command in our text. Earlier in the chapter he enjoins us to "walk in the Spirit" (verse 16), but here in verses 22 and 23 there is no hint of a command. In other places the virtues here listed are commanded. We are told to love God and our neighbor, to rejoice in the Lord, and to "be at peace among yourselves" (1 Thessalonians 5:13). Indeed, all the virtues mentioned in Galatians 5:22–23 are commanded somewhere in the Bible. In our text, however, they are not presented as duties, but as the fruit of the Spirit. This fact carries many valuable lessons.

The first lesson is that Christian character is not the result of good habits. In fact the reverse is the case: our good habits are the result of Christian character. This is in keeping with the entire tenor of Paul's message to the Galatians, which strongly emphasizes that salvation is not by works, but by grace through faith alone.

The second lesson is that God must work holiness in us before we can work it out in Christian living. Before there can be fruit there must be a root. The root of all practical holiness, or *sanctification,* is regeneration. Until the Holy Spirit quickens our dead souls we cannot produce any spiritual fruit, but remain "dead in trespasses and sins" (Ephesians 2:1). Thus the Spirit's act of regeneration precedes all the virtues mentioned in our text. As Paul wrote to the Philippians, "Work out your own salvation with fear and trembling. For it is God which worketh in you both to will and to do of his good pleasure" (Philippians 2:12–13).

A third important lesson is that God produces holiness in every regenerate soul. The regenerating act of the Spirit of God bears fruit. He does not labor in vain. Thus the apostle John says, "Whosoever is born of God doth not commit sin; for his seed remaineth in him: and he cannot sin, because he is born of God" (1 John 3:9). John's message here is the same as Paul's in our text. Christian holiness is the result of regeneration (i.e., being born of God) and of what new birth produces; it is a genuine, ongoing experience of the Holy Spirit's operations in the soul. It is that ongoing experience that John describes as God's seed remaining in us.

A fourth lesson is that it is this ongoing work of the Spirit that gives us the power to be holy. It should come as no surprise that the Holy Spirit is the author of holiness in God's people. Nowhere is it more true than in the battle against sin that it is "not by might, nor by power, but by my spirit, saith the Lord of hosts" (Zechariah 4:6).

Fruit, Not the Works of the Flesh

The second observation we must make is that Paul speaks of the fruit of the Spirit, not the product of the flesh. As we have just noted, victory over sin is "by my spirit, saith the Lord of hosts." In concrete terms what does this mean? It surely means two things: first, that Christian virtue is produced by the activity of the Holy Spirit within a believer, and second, that the fruit the Holy Spirit produces is truly spiritual fruit.

Christian Virtue Is Produced by the Holy Spirit's Work

The activity of the Spirit within a Christian is what produces Christian virtue in him. Christian virtue and character are not products of human effort or will power. They are not the results of some program of self-help. The Bible never drives a man to dig deep within himself to find the resources he needs to be the kind of person God wants him to be. Rather it tells him that however deep he digs, he will find nothing in himself but spiritual corruption. As Paul said, "I know that in me (that is, in my flesh,) dwelleth no good thing" (Romans 7:18). But the same apostle could rejoice that "if the Spirit of him that raised up Jesus from the dead dwell in you, he that raised up Christ from the dead shall also quicken your mortal bodies by his Spirit that dwelleth in you" (Romans 8:11). In other words, the indwelling of the Holy Spirit in a believer is real and effective.

The Spirit is the author or agent of our sanctification (2 Thessalonians 2:13). He dwells in all true believers (Romans 8:9) and He acts in all in whom He dwells. The New Testament is full of what the Holy Spirit does in and for believers, as we shall see. "The fruit of the Spirit" is a summary description of the work He carries on, a beautifully complete statement of the virtue and character He works to produce in His people. So in dealing with this fruit of the Spirit we are considering not some work of the flesh, but what the Holy Ghost produces in and through us by His activity.

That raises a question: Precisely what is the activity of the Spirit that produces the fruit of which Paul speaks? We may highlight three actions of the Spirit that are of particular significance.

The first is His exposure of sin. By exposing our sin the Spirit guides us away from what is grieving to Him and harmful to us. He shows us the right course to take. His word is like a sword that pierces the deepest recesses of our being (Hebrews 4:12). The Holy Spirit dwelling within us does not connive at sin. He does not play along with us in our fleshly attempts to justify sin. He turns the light of His word on our hearts, exposing what is wrong in our lives and showing us how God expects us to live.

The Holy Spirit's second activity is His revelation of Christ to us. This is His special work, the fundamental reason for His coming as the Comforter (John 16:14). Paul prayed for the Ephesian believers "that the God of our Lord Jesus Christ, the Father of glory, may give unto you the spirit of wisdom and revelation in the knowledge of him: the eyes of your understanding being enlightened" (Ephesians 1:17–18). By revealing Christ to us, the Holy Spirit creates in us a desire to follow Him, not out of mere duty, but out of faith in and love for Christ. Nothing so stimulates a believer as a sight of His Saviour. The more our lives are a reaction to the love of God in Christ and to our standing in Him as those who are fully justified on the ground of His imputed righteousness and thus accepted by the Father, the holier and happier we will be.

The Spirit's third activity in producing fruit in the lives of believers is His control of His people. By controlling and governing us the Spirit subdues the passions of our flesh and stirs our hearts to desire the Lord as Asaph did: "Whom have I in heaven but thee? and there is none upon earth that I desire beside thee" (Psalm 73:25). The Spirit gives us the ability to keep looking to Christ and to keep reacting in a spiritual manner to all our varied circumstances, so that we live as the hymn says, "above the world and sin, with hearts made pure and garments white and Christ enthroned within."

This is a control we must willingly accept, as is clear from the command, "Be not drunk with wine, wherein is excess; but be filled with the Spirit" (Ephesians 5:18). This is our duty as Christians. We should live under the Spirit's control just as certainly as a drunkard lives under the control of alcohol. There are striking contrasts between being drunk and being full of the Spirit, but there is one clear parallel. We speak of someone who is drunk as being under the influence—that is, the control—of alcohol. It governs how he thinks, speaks, perceives, feels, and acts. Similarly, a person who is full of the Holy Spirit is under His influence or control. The Spirit governs his attitudes and actions just as surely as alcohol does those of the drunkard. That is another way of saying that the Holy Spirit *leads* God's people. But again we must stress the need for the believer's willing acceptance of the Spirit's work. The Spirit's leading supposes our following, that is, that we heartily submit to His guidance and yield to His control. This caution is necessary. We must not imagine that the activity of the Spirit lifts us out of the daily battle with sin or removes from us the responsibility of confronting our sinful flesh. Far from it, but what it does is to enable us to make the choice of faith to submit to His leading. To the extent we obey the command of Ephesians 5:18 we will experience the liberating control of God's Spirit in our lives.

To the carnal mind nothing is more obnoxious than the thought of being under the control of God's Spirit. Sinners pride themselves that they exercise *free* will. They deride the idea of divine government as something that reduces us to the level of puppets. Nothing could be further from the truth. For a start, sinners are not free at all. Their vaunted freedom of will is freedom to be slaves to sin and Satan. They act according to the prevailing disposition of their will, which is always sinful and selfish, and they are energized by "the prince of the power of the air," the devil (Ephesians 2:1–3). Christians have a different disposition of will that directs their choices. They desire to please God. To them godliness is freedom and the gracious work of the Holy Spirit in governing and controlling them is something they fully and freely embrace, because it is to them the very essence of liberty. They realize the truth of the hymn, "Make me a captive, Lord, and then I shall be free."

The Holy Spirit uses certain means to further this work of grace in His people. The first is *the word of God*. That is why Christians should be daily diligent in their study of the Scriptures. The Spirit guides us through the word: "Thy word is a lamp unto my feet, and a light unto my path" (Psalm 119:105). He uses the Scriptures to alert us to moral and spiritual danger: "By them is thy servant warned" (Psalm 19:11). He also feeds and strengthens us by His word. Thus Job said, "I have esteemed the words of his mouth more than my necessary food" (Job 23:12; see Jeremiah 15:16; Ezekiel 3:1–3; Psalm 19:10; 119:72). All this makes not only our personal reading of Scripture vitally important, but also our attendance on the preaching of the word. "The preaching of the cross is to them that perish foolishness; but unto us which are saved it is the power of God" (1 Corinthians 1:18). Paul tells us that God has "manifested his word through preaching" (Titus 1:3). Every time we go to hear the preaching of God's word—which should be frequently, but at least each Lord's Day—we should pray as Eli directed Samuel, "Speak, Lord; for thy servant heareth" (1 Samuel 3:9).

Prayer is another means the Spirit employs in our sanctification. The activity of the Spirit is more obvious here, perhaps, than anywhere else, for left to ourselves we cannot pray. "Because our abilities are far from able to match" what is required in true prayer, "therefore, in order to minister to this weakness, God gives us the spirit as our teacher" (John Calvin, *Institutes,* 3.20:5). As Paul said, "The Spirit also helpeth our infirmities: for we know not what we should pray for as we ought: but the Spirit itself maketh intercession for us with groanings which cannot be uttered" (Romans 8:26). Calvin rightly interprets this groaning of the Spirit as part of His sanctifying work in us: "Not that he actually prays or groans but arouses in us assurance, desires, and sighs, to conceive which our natural powers would scarcely suffice."

A third means the Spirit uses to sanctify us is *the ministry of the church and of our fellow Christians.* The church is "the pillar and ground of the truth" (1 Timothy 3:15). As long as a church remains true to this calling as a supporter and sustainer of God's revealed truth, we should "hear the church," as the Lord Jesus put it (Matthew 18:17). Our risen Lord "gave some, apostles; and some, prophets; and some, evangelists; and some, pastors and teachers; for the perfecting of the saints, for the work of the ministry, for the edifying of the body of Christ" (Ephesians 4:11–12). Church worship and fellowship are not optional extras for God's people, but necessary means of promoting spiritual maturity. Proverbs 27:17 tells us, "Iron sharpeneth iron; so a man sharpeneth the countenance of his friend." As they enter into genuine gospel fellowship, Christians edify and are edified by their brethren. Thus it is the will of our Saviour that "speaking the truth in love, [we] may grow up into him in all things, which is the head, even Christ" (Ephesians 4:15). By this loving interaction among His people the Holy Spirit opens both the hearts and mouths of believers to each other, ministering needed grace to them.

As Christians we are not self-sufficient. We need each other for that is how God has designed the development of His church. What a responsibility this places on us! It is a responsibility to walk with God and to live in fellowship with Him so that we can carry a word from Him to some needy believer. And it is a responsibility to be humble enough to listen to what our brethren say to us, always, of course, subjecting their words to the standard of Scripture.

We may mention a final means the Spirit often uses to sanctify us: *affliction*. The Bible tells us plainly that affliction is never a pleasant experience. "No chastening for the present seemeth to be joyous, but grievous: nevertheless afterward it yieldeth the peaceable fruit of righteousness unto them which are exercised thereby" (Hebrews 12:11). It was because he had proved the sanctifying benefits of affliction that the psalmist stated, "It is good for me that I have been afflicted; that I might learn thy statutes" (Psalms 119:71).

This is how the Holy Spirit produces His fruit in our lives. By these various means He leads us to confess and repent of the sin He exposes. He leads us to a fresh exercise of faith in Christ our Saviour and to a humble, hearty submission to the will of God.

The Holy Spirit Produces Spiritual Fruit

In establishing that the virtues Paul lists in Galatians 5:22–23 are the fruit of the Spirit, not the product of the flesh, we have shown that it is the activity of the Holy Spirit within a believer that produces this fruit. Now we must emphasize the second line of thought mentioned earlier: The fruit that the Holy Spirit produces is always spiritual fruit. This truth is so obvious that it is often overlooked. It is important for us not to make that mistake. When speaking of virtue and character, most people content themselves with externals. They pay attention to the attitudes and actions discernible by others. These are certainly important matters and it is obvious that true Christian virtue and character will powerfully form our attitudes and actions. But the point to grasp is that Christian virtue and character are what Peter terms "the hidden man of the heart" (1 Peter 3:4). This hidden man is the internal foundation for such outward manifestations as our attitudes and actions.

As Christians we can never be satisfied with externals. The Lord looks on the heart and we feel the necessity of being "strengthened with might by his Spirit in the inner man" (Ephesians 3:16). It is understandable for unregenerate people to be satisfied with mere behavior modifications, for that is as far as man can go. But the Holy Spirit goes deeper and deals with our inmost souls. His work is to change and fashion the deepest characteristics of the soul. Paul traces the commencement of this moral and spiritual revolution to the work of God by His Spirit in making the believer a new creation in Christ: "The new man . . . after [the likeness of] God is created in righteousness and true holiness" (Ephesians 4:24). Paul further describes this moral and spiritual revolution as an ongoing, internal transformation: "Be not conformed to this world: but be ye transformed by the renewing of your mind, that ye may prove what is that good, and acceptable, and perfect, will of God" (Romans 12:2).

This is the fruit of the Spirit. Anything else is not. All that savors of self or of the world is not the product of the Holy Spirit. This simple observation, if they would only stop to consider it, would save many professing Christians from seriously sinful behavior. If they did so, when they contemplate obviously unscriptural actions or decisions they could not persuade themselves, as unfortunately many do, that they are acting under the leading of the Spirit. Any time we claim His leading we should remember that His fruit is spiritual, never carnal.

A Ninefold Description of One Indivisible Fruit

The third major observation we must make from our text is that Paul speaks of one indivisible fruit in nine particulars—love, joy, peace, longsuffering, gentleness, goodness, faith, meekness, and temperance. None of the virtues he mentions can exist alone. Each leads to the others. Love, first to God and then to others, satisfies the soul and naturally leads to joy or delight in our Saviour and His salvation. This joy yields peace, that is, a sense of security and assurance in Christ that gives the quality of tranquility or serenity to life. Peace enables us to exhibit longsuffering: if we are at peace with ourselves we will be patient with others. We will therefore show gentleness or kindness, which in turn will manifest goodness, or a character of moral worth that seeks to do good. Any person who displays such spiritual fruit will always face difficulty and opposition in this world of sin and trouble. He will need the grace of faith, or faithfulness and firm continuance in His godliness. If we enjoy the fruit so far described, we will certainly not lack this firmness of commitment to Christ. This faithfulness, though it will be sorely tested by life's adversities, will render us meek, for meekness is a submissive acceptance of God's sovereign dealings with us. Meekness will in turn produce temperance, or a life of self-control, not one blown about by all the changing pressures we encounter.

The Fruit of the Spirit Is Christlikeness

What Paul describes in these nine virtues is a life wholly conformed to the image of Christ. The Lord Jesus Christ is the perfection and personification of all the virtues that constitute the fruit of the Spirit, because God gave Him the Spirit without measure (John 3:34). Thus the aim of the Spirit's work in us is to make us like Christ. Indeed this is God's eternal purpose in saving us, for He predestinated us "to be conformed to the image of His Son" (Romans 8:29). Thus, likeness to Christ is the Holy Spirit's objective as He pursues our moral and spiritual transformation. This was the message Paul brought to the early churches: "We all, with open face beholding as in a glass the glory of the Lord, are changed into the same image from glory to glory, even as by the Spirit of the Lord" (2 Corinthians 3:18). To the Galatians, who were being ensnared by false teachers into a false gospel and a false spiritual experience, he wrote: "My little children, . . . I travail in birth again [for you] until Christ be formed in you" (Galatians 4:19). This is the great aim of the Spirit in all His workings with us: conformity to Christ. Nothing less will do. This is the fruit of the Spirit par excellence.

Fruitfulness Depends on the State of the Heart

We must make one final observation: The quality and quantity of the fruit of the Spirit that any of us experiences depends in large measure on the state of the heart out of which it grows. Our hearts are like soil in which a farmer sows his seed. It is not the quality of the seed alone that determines the harvest. The state of the soil is a major factor. Thus the Bible tells us that we have the responsibility to purify our hearts and to respond wholeheartedly to the Holy Spirit's work in us: "Thus saith the Lord . . . Break up your fallow ground, and sow not among thorns" (Jeremiah 4:3). The Song of Solomon likens the church to "a garden inclosed" (4:12). Men plant gardens to produce a harvest and God cultivates our souls with the same purpose. He has made us so that we may bring forth fruit.

We do not all produce the same quality and quantity of fruit, as the Lord Jesus made clear in His parable of the seed falling into good ground. Some Christians bring forth "an hundredfold, some sixtyfold, some thirtyfold" (Matthew 13:8, 23). However, though we do not all bear the same amount of fruit, all true Christians bear *some* fruit. Professing Christians who bear *no* fruit are unsaved. Their profession is empty and hypocritical. They are like the fruitless fig tree in Christ's parable: they cumber the ground and will be cut down in judgment unless they repent and bring forth "fruits meet for repentance" (Luke 13:6–9; Matthew 3:7–8; Acts 26:20). True believers are altogether different. Of them Jesus says, "Ye have not chosen me, but I have chosen you, and ordained you, that ye should go and bring forth fruit, and that your fruit should remain" (John 15:16). Because they have the Spirit of God dwelling in them they produce some real spiritual fruit. It cannot be otherwise.

We must not be satisfied to produce minimal fruit. It is the will of God that we "bring forth more fruit" (John 15:2). The Holy Spirit abides within us to make us fruitful. To experience the mighty working of His power we should attend to the command of God recorded in Hosea 10:12: "Sow to yourselves in righteousness, reap in mercy; break up your fallow ground: for it is time to seek the Lord, till he come and rain righteousness upon you."

Love, the First Fruit of the Spirit

"The fruit of the Spirit is love."
Galatians 5:22

The most terrible indictment that God can make of any man is the one the Lord Jesus made of the Jews: "I know you that you have not the love of God in you" (John 5:42). Paul described the dreadful consequences of this state in 1 Corinthians 16:22: "If any man love not the Lord Jesus Christ, let him be anathema." The apostle John added an equally strong denunciation: "If any man love the world, the love of the Father is not in him" (1 John 2:15). These Scriptures teach that a soul without the love of God is bereft of all true spiritual life. It is yet dead in trespasses and sins, alienated from the life of God through the wickedness that is in it, corrupt and condemned.

In striking contrast to all this, Paul asserts, "The fruit of the Spirit is love." Because love is the fruit of the Spirit, it is the product of life. Where this love is, there is the undeniable evidence of true life, that is, of eternal life. The *existence* of this fruit arises from the gracious regenerating act of the Holy Spirit. The *cultivation* or *abundance* of it arises from His sanctifying, or life-sustaining, work. Standing at the head of the imposing list of virtues in Galatians 5:22–23, love is in some ways the sum of all the rest. That is why Paul sets forth love as the first fruit of the Spirit.

The First Christian Virtue

Paul places love at the head of the list of virtues that constitute the fruit of the Spirit because love is the first virtue that the Holy Spirit produces in His progressive work in a believer. Love is not the first *work* that the Holy Ghost performs in us. Conviction and effectual calling precede it. However, as to the *fruit* of the Spirit in regenerated people, love comes first. It is the first virtue that the Holy Spirit produces in the life of a true believer. We may mark three distinct actions by which the Spirit produces this fruit.

The Spirit Produces Love in Us by Witnessing to God's Love for Us

The first action by which the Holy Spirit produces the fruit of love in believers is by His witnessing to us of the love of God for us. "The love of God is shed abroad [poured forth] in our hearts by the Holy Ghost which is given unto us" (Romans 5:5).

He witnesses to us of the love of the Father in sovereign election and in the covenant of grace. He makes the revelation of God's eternal purpose a sweet truth that warms our hearts. To the carnal mind the thought of a God who elects is an insult to man's claim to autonomy. Man wants to occupy the throne. If he could, he would reduce God to the level of the puppet of the all-powerful human will. The carnal mind detests any doctrine that levels the pride of flesh in the dust and says that there is a God in heaven who owes no man any favor and who sovereignly and eternally chooses His people. But this is the very truth that the Holy Spirit brings with sweetness to our hearts. God in grace has chosen a people whom He has given to His Son in the covenant of grace. He has appointed Christ to be their mediator, through whose life, death, resurrection, and intercession He will bring them to glory.

The Spirit also witnesses of the love of the Son in making atonement for the sins of His people. He constantly points God's people to Calvary, and in the bleeding wounds of Christ—in the thorn-crowned brow, the broken heart, the outpoured blood, the finished work of the cross—He shows them the indescribable love of Christ. Thus they can say with Paul, "The Son of God . . . loved me, and gave himself for me" (Galatians 2:20).

Then the Spirit witnesses of His own love to us in regenerating and indwelling us. The Scriptures do not speak much of the love of the Spirit as distinct from the love of the Father and of the Son. But God—in the Trinity of His sacred persons—loves us, and that includes the Holy Spirit. In Romans 15:30 we read of Paul's exhorting the believers by "the love of the Spirit" to pray for him. While most commentators interpret this as the love the Spirit causes us to have one for another, Matthew Henry is right in including the Spirit's own love for us: "If ever you experienced the Spirit's love to you, and would be found returning your love to the Spirit, be not wanting in this office of kindness." By every revelation that He gives us through the Bible and with every application of it to our hearts, the Holy Spirit evidences His love for us. He witnesses to us, "I regenerated you, because I loved you. I sanctify you, even when it is through affliction, because I love you. I indwell you because I love you." Thus, love is the first fruit of the Spirit because the Spirit witnesses to us of the love of God for us.

The Spirit Produces Love in Us by Giving Us a Love for God

The second action by which the Holy Spirit produces the fruit of love in believers is this: by witnessing to God's love for us He produces in us a love for God. Love for God is the first and natural result of the Holy Spirit's regeneration of our souls and of His consequent revelation of Christ in our hearts. When He regenerates us, He makes us new creatures. The evidence of this fundamental change is that He gives us a new outlook. As new creatures we now repent of sin. Repentance is the most clear, unmistakable evidence of a new nature that the Bible speaks about. Before conversion, men's minds are darkened and their wills depraved. Love of self governs their souls. They make everything to serve the interests of self. Sinners would even reduce Almighty God to the level of their slave if they could. That is the definitive mark of the unconverted. Even the kindness and goodness of a sinful man always terminate upon man, usually upon himself. But regeneration changes all this. Once God saves a man He causes such a revolution in his will that its entire bias or disposition becomes fixed on God.

Repentance is more than sorrow for sin or a determination to forsake it. It includes these elements, but it goes much deeper. In giving us repentance, the Holy Spirit creates a fundamental alteration in the bias of our will *away* from loving and serving self and *toward* loving and serving God—just as in giving us the gift of saving faith He creates a fundamental alteration in the disposition of the will away from trusting in self and our own merits to trusting in Christ and His merits. So, instead of making our own glory or pleasure the chief end of our being, we now set before us the God of glory and make Him the one for whom we live.

When He regenerates us, the Holy Spirit not only renews our wills, He also enlightens our minds so that we can think straight for the first time in our lives. We see everything in a new light. The hymn writer tried to describe this enlightened mind:

> Heav'n above is softer blue,
> Earth around is sweeter green!
> Something lives in every hue
> Christless eyes have never seen:
> Birds with gladder songs o'erflow,
> Flowers with deeper beauty shine,
> Since I know, as now I know,
> I am His, and He is mine.

Now we think of God as we never thought of Him before. We see Christ in an entirely new light. We look at ourselves as we never did before. We think of eternity as we never thought of it before. We can now think God's thoughts after Him. There was a time when we dismissed Christ with contempt, fulfilling Isaiah's prophecy: "He hath no form nor comeliness; and when we shall see him, there is no beauty that we should desire him. He is despised and rejected of men; a man of sorrows, and acquainted with grief: and we hid as it were our faces from him; he was despised, and we esteemed him not" (Isaiah 53:2–3).

Now, however, after the Spirit has regenerated us and shown us God's love for us, we are filled with gratitude. With Solomon we say of Christ, "Yea, he is altogether lovely" (Song of Solomon 5:16). With John the apostle we confess, "We love him, because he first loved us" (1 John 4:19). With the psalmist we testify, "I love the Lord, because he hath heard my voice and my supplications. Because he hath inclined his ear unto me, therefore will I call upon him as long as I live. The sorrows of death compassed me, and the pains of hell gat hold upon me: I found trouble and sorrow. Then called I upon the name of the Lord; O Lord, I beseech thee, deliver my soul. Gracious is the Lord, and righteous; yea, our God is merciful" (Psalm 116:1–5). Awakened to see God's love for our souls, we exclaim with Paul, "Thanks be unto God for his unspeakable gift" (2 Corinthians 9:15).

Then the Spirit stirs us to desire God. Nothing else satisfies. "Whom have I in heaven but thee? and there is none upon earth that I desire beside thee" (Psalm 73:25). Every true Christian desires Christ. Yet every one of us laments that we do not love Him enough. We do not love Him with the depth, passion, and feeling that we think we ought to feel. As a result we often conclude that we must not really love Him at all. However, the desire for Christ is an exercise of love, the fruit of the Spirit.

Love is seen in its yearning—even in the confession of its inadequacy—as truly as in its moments of exhilaration. Only a Christian can say, "There is none upon the earth that I desire beside thee." With the witness of God's love within us we long for His fellowship, and this desire is an evidence of the fruit of the Sprit. We may feel that we cannot pray very well, but we feel compelled to pray nevertheless. We may mourn that our faith does not perceive Christ clearly enough as we study the Scriptures, yet we read on, feeling that we must get a glimpse of Him. This is the fruit of the Holy Spirit. He witnesses of God's love for us and consequently produces in us a love for God.

The Spirit Produces Love in Us by Giving Us a Love Like God's Love

The Holy Spirit does even more than produce in us a love for God: He produces in us a love like God's love. When the Holy Spirit imparts this first fruit to us, *we begin to love what God loves.* "The righteous Lord loveth righteousness" (Psalm 11:7). Those who have the love of God in them will therefore love righteousness. They will love what God loves and hate what God hates.

They will love those whom God loves. Whom does God love? For a start, He loves His people, and all who have His love in them will love His people too. "By this shall all men know that ye are my disciples, if ye have love one to another" (John 13:35). People who say that they love God and hate the saints are deluding themselves. "If a man say, I love God, and hateth his brother, he is a liar: for he that loveth not his brother whom he hath seen, how can he love God whom he hath not seen?" (1 John 4:20).

God also loves sinners. We must never pervert the glorious truth of God's sovereign, electing grace or of Christ's particular redemption of His covenant people in such a way as to diminish our view of the greatness of the heart of God toward a world of sinners. He loves the ungodly. How and why he loves sinners we cannot tell, but he loves them and so should we. How can we, sinners whom He has loved and saved, love Him but despise perishing sinners? How can we love the great lover of sinners and yet act like Pharisees, treating their spiritual state with careless indifference, showing no concern for their souls as they rush on to destruction? The fruit of the Spirit is love and those who have the love of God in them will love those whom God loves.

They will love as God loves. God loves redemptively. The great aim of His love is the salvation of the lost: "God so loved the world, that he gave his only begotten Son, that whosoever believeth in him should not perish, but have everlasting life" (John 3:16). "Herein is love, not that we loved God, but that he loved us, and sent his Son to be the propitiation for our sins" (1 John 4:10). Our love for souls must reflect this redemptive love of God. We cannot save souls, but in love we may tell them of the One who can. We cannot satisfy our consciences or truly show forth the love of God by doing anything less.

All our humanitarian deeds, such as feeding the hungry and clothing the destitute, are good and worthy Christian endeavors. If we stop there, however, we fail to love as God loves. He feeds and clothes the needy, but these mercies are not ends in themselves; they are designed to call to Christ those who receive them. By failing to keep the redemptive aspect of Christian love in view, many have fallen into the folly of the liberals, who limit the expression of love to social action. It is a hollow kind of love that offers a man better food, better clothing, better housing, or better education while denying him the message of saving grace—the only means by which he may pass from eternal death into eternal life.

Historically, Bible-believing Christians have been in the vanguard of every movement to improve the earthly lot of the poor and needy. When William Booth was serving the Lord in the slums of London he said that it was a waste of time for him to talk about the way to heaven to a man whose stomach was hungry, whose children were starving, and whose pockets were empty. The Bible makes it clear that we cannot turn our eyes away from such needs. It also makes it clear that addressing such needs is not the gospel. It is not the fundamental mission of the church of Christ on earth. If we love as God loves we must love men to Christ. We must bring to them the glorious message of redeeming grace and of full salvation through faith in Christ's atonement. That is how God loves, with a redemptive love.

Those in whom the Holy Spirit produces the first fruit of love will love not only what He loves, whom He loves, and as He loves. *They will also love for the same reason He loves, which is for His glory.* The Lord says, "I, even I, am he that blotteth out thy transgressions for mine own sake, and will not remember thy sins" (Isaiah 43:25). The great motivation for the love of God is the divine glory. The same is true in those who have the first fruit of the Spirit. We love saints and sinners for the glory of God. That puts a whole new aspect on how we relate to people. We do not love them because they deserve it, or because they have something attractive about them. We do not love them merely by the exercise of our own kindly disposition. We love them because we seek to bring glory to God as the result of our ministry to them. That will enable us to love even the most unlovely.

Years ago I read a true story that really challenged me. A preacher in England was doing his best to reach needy people with the gospel, and with some success. Despite his best efforts, however, there was one particularly vile, foul-mouthed drunkard with whom he found it very difficult to get along. This man despised the preacher and his message and he made no secret of it. He was quite happy to receive free food when it was offered, but he wanted nothing to do with the gospel. Many a time the preacher told him of the love of God. For his trouble the old fellow cursed him. Going back to his room, the preacher went to his closet before God and began to pray for that man. As he prayed God challenged him, "Have you given him the message of love?" The preacher replied to the Lord, "Lord, you know I have given him the gospel." But the Lord was insistent in speaking to his conscience: "I did not ask you if you had told him the gospel. Have you told him that you love him?" The preacher sought a way of escape from his troubled thoughts but finally recognized that for all his preaching to the old sinner he had no love for him. Finally, after a long time of agonizing in prayer, he felt God touch his heart and give him a love for that foul sinner. He went out to look for the man and found him just as smelly and obnoxious as ever. But it was a new preacher who met him. Instead of standing at arm's length and telling him that God loved him, he went right up to him and put his arm around him and told him of the love of Christ again. This time he could honestly add, "I love you, too." The old man was stunned and soon was on his knees crying to God for mercy. The preacher had learned to look beyond the old sinner's hatefulness and catch a sight of how God would be glorified in his conversion to Christ. Let us keep the glory of God before us and we will be free to love with a love like God's love.

Love is the fundamental fruit of the Spirit in believers. As yet, the work of producing it in us is not perfected. It has begun, but it has not been completed. We are not yet what we ought to be. Nevertheless, the Holy Spirit has begun to produce this fruit within us. It is a real work that He is doing, one that is fundamental to every other work of grace in us. This is why it stands at the head of the list of those virtues that constitute the fruit of the Spirit.

Love, the Antithesis and Answer to the Flesh

The Holy Spirit makes love the antithesis and the answer to all the works of the flesh. That is why it is at the head of the list of virtues. In Gala-tians 5:16 Paul says that the flesh lusts against the Spirit. In verses 19 through 21 he describes "the works of the flesh" by which it carries out this warfare: "Now the works of the flesh are manifest, which are these; Adultery, fornication, uncleanness, lasciviousness, idolatry, witchcraft, hatred, variance, emulations, wrath, strife, seditions, here-sies, envyings, murders, drunkenness, revellings, and such like." Now in verse 22 the apostle makes love the first fruit of the Spirit's work in us. Why? Surely, it is because this love stands in opposition to all "the works of the flesh." Every one of them is a perversion of love in one form or another. Adultery, fornication, uncleanness, and lasciviousness are perversions of domestic and marital love. Idolatry and witchcraft are perversions of love for God. Hatred, variance, emulations, wrath, strifes, and seditions are perversions of love for the brethren. Heresies are perversions of the love for truth. Envyings and murders are perversions of the love we should have for others, while drunkenness, revel-lings, and such like are perversions of the love that we ought to have for our own souls and happiness.

All these works of the flesh stand in antithesis to love and love stands in antithesis to them. In every case the work of the flesh flourishes because of a failure of love—not merely a failure of love to man, but to God. For example, why do people commit adultery, fornication, uncleanness, and lasciviousness? We may answer, "Because they don't love their spouses enough." That is true, but it is not the whole truth or even the most funda-mental truth. The real answer is that they do not love the Lord enough.

Seeing the works of the flesh as a failure of love enables us to grasp an important truth: The love of the Spirit is the answer to all the works of the flesh and by it He supplies the power to overcome them. What is the answer for a person who is struggling with any one of these per-versions? Christ is the answer. Let that person know the love of Christ for him, let his heart be stirred to love Christ, and he will receive the power to become an overcomer in any of these areas of conflict with the flesh. We cannot live in immorality while we are in love with Christ. We cannot fall into idolatry, witchcraft, or heresies, or into hatred, variance, emulations, wrath, strifes, seditions, envyings, or murders if our hearts are filled with love to Christ. Not only will we love God but we will love sinners, we will love the saints, and we will love our families. We will enjoy proper relationships in all these areas if only the love of the Spirit springs up in our hearts.

Here is the answer to every lust of the flesh. The fruit of the Spirit is love. As Paul said in a slightly different connection, "For the love of Christ constraineth us" (2 Corinthians 5:14). In a preeminent sense this means that His love for us controls and impels us to serve Him. There is no greater motivational power for a Christian to do right than to know the love of God for him and thus to feel a love for God stirring up in him. This is the answer to the works of the flesh. That is why love stands at the top of the list of the virtues that constitute the fruit of the Spirit.

The Source of All Other Virtues

Paul places love first because the Holy Spirit makes this love the source of all the virtues that follow. The apostle lists nine aspects of the fruit of the Spirit and every one of them is the direct result of the first. Love produces joy, peace, longsuffering, gentleness, goodness, faith, meekness, and temperance. That renders it surpassingly important. The more the Spirit produces His first fruit of love in us the more He will enable us to bring forth all the rest of His fruit. This is the power of love. Gripped with this truth Samuel Rutherford cried, "I think it is possible on earth to build a young New Jerusalem, a little new heaven, of this surpassing love. God, either send me more of this love, or take me quickly over the water, where I may be filled with his love."

Joy in the Holy Ghost

"The fruit of the Spirit is . . . joy."
Galatians 5:22

With a typically terse and beautiful statement Thomas Watson contrasted the eternal life Christians experience now with what they will experience in heaven: "Here joy begins to enter into us; there we enter into joy." As Christians, we do not doubt that all true believers will enter into joy. Why then do we find it so difficult to accept that when we are saved, joy enters into us? It is clear that many Christians do find this difficult to accept for they openly lament that they have little or no joy. They fear a text such as Galatians 5:22, which states emphatically, "The fruit of the Spirit is joy," because they rightly conclude from it that if a person is a genuine Christian he will have joy and anyone without joy cannot be a Christian. To any Bible believer's conscience this logic is irresistible. However, a believer in Christ need not fear the statement of Galatians 5:22 that the Holy Ghost produces joy in those whom He unites to Christ. Let me give you a word of explanation, followed by a word of encouragement, and then a word of exhortation to show you why.

A Word of Explanation

Let us start with a word of explanation. Some time ago I received a telephone call from a church elder in another city. He said, "I have been doing some Bible study and have been trying to find a good definition of joy. I have not been satisfied with what I have been able to find in my commentaries and Bible dictionary. Can you define joy for me?" That was quite a challenge for *joy* is one of those words that almost everyone imagines he perfectly understands, but does not. When we seek to define *joy* the first word that usually springs to mind is *happiness*. Unfortunately, this is the wrong word entirely, and it sends us off on a false track. Happiness is associated with what is happening to us; joy goes much deeper and, transcending what is happening, settles our pleasure on a much more solid foundation. In the general sense, joy is the pleasure a person feels at the remembrance, possession, or prospect of something he believes to be of value. Spiritual joy is that pleasure lifted up to a much higher plane. We will define it in three ways.

Joy Defined

First, *spiritual joy is the response of a believer to the understanding the Holy Spirit communicates to him of God's love to him in Christ.* Joy is a response to knowing that God loves us. The certainty that God is our Saviour produces real joy, whatever our immediate circumstances may be. In her wonderful song, the Magnificat, the Virgin Mary exulted, "My spirit hath rejoiced in God my Saviour" (Luke 1:47). A person who is convinced that the God of heaven is his personal Saviour will naturally react with a sense of deep satisfaction and pleasure. The knowledge of the love of God our Father must have this effect.

Second, *spiritual joy is also the delight a Christian takes in the position, possessions, and prospects that he has in Christ.* Think of our *position* in Him. The key phrase in Ephesians is "in Christ," a phrase that first and foremost defines our position. Once we were "without Christ," but now we are "in Christ." Paul describes the wonder of this union in many places, but never more beautifully than in Ephesians 2:4–6: "God, who is rich in mercy, for his great love wherewith he loved us, even when we were dead in sins, hath quickened us together with Christ, (by grace ye are saved;) and hath raised us up together, and made us sit together in heavenly places in Christ Jesus."

So even while they are still on earth, facing all the struggles that life presents, believers have been raised up together with Christ and made to sit in heavenly places in Him. What is it to be in Christ? It is to be so united to Christ that what He is legally and covenantally (that is, as the covenant head of His people) in God's sight, we are in Him. Where He is, we are in Him. That is what it is to be united to Christ. God looks on Christ and His believing people as being one body. Christ is the head and believers are the members of that body. God will never sunder the mystical body of His Son. He will never deal with Christ apart from His people and He will never deal with His people apart from Christ. This is our position, and by convincing us of it, the Holy Spirit produces spiritual joy in us.

He does so also by showing us our *possessions* in Christ. The assurance of union with Christ opens up to a believer the glorious scope of these possessions. Passages such as Ephesians chapter one and 1 Peter 1:2–6 set these forth in considerable detail. In Christ we have received the blessings of divine election, predestination, adoption, redemption, and the gift of the Holy Spirit as the seal of God's securing of our souls for eternity. By witnessing to us of the riches of God's gracious provision for us in Christ the Holy Spirit makes us to rejoice. Paul said, "We . . . joy in God through our Lord Jesus Christ, by whom we have now received the atonement [or reconciliation]" (Romans 5:11). Jesus told his disciples, "In this rejoice not, that the spirits are subject unto you; but rather rejoice, because your names are written in heaven" (Luke 10:20).

The Holy Spirit also makes us glad by witnessing to the *prospects* that God opens to us because of Christ's work on our behalf. As Peter puts it, we "are kept by the power of God through faith unto salvation ready to be revealed in the last time" (1 Peter 1:5). Eternal glory awaits every believer: "Rejoice, inasmuch as ye are partakers of Christ's sufferings; that, when his glory shall be revealed, ye may be glad also with exceeding joy" (1 Peter 4:13). Even the severest afflictions cannot dim this hope of glory. Indeed, Paul tells us that they are in some ways like birth pangs preparatory to the realization of that hope: "Our light affliction, which is but for a moment, worketh for us a far more exceeding and eternal weight of glory" (2 Corinthians 4:17). Laying hold of these truths will always gladden a believing soul.

Third, spiritual joy is the gladness a Christian experiences because of the Holy Spirit's indwelling and continuing work of grace in his heart. Thus Paul defined the experience of the true subjects of Christ's kingdom in the following terms: "The kingdom of God is . . . righteousness, and peace, and joy in the Holy Ghost" (Romans 14:17).

I have deliberately given a Trinitarian emphasis in this triple definition of joy. Joy is our response to the fact that our Father loves us. It is our delight at our union with Christ, God's incarnate Son. It is our gladness at the indwelling and sanctifying work of the Holy Spirit in our hearts. Now we have begun to understand a little of what joy is. At this stage it would be beneficial to take a good concordance and assemble the pieces for a detailed word study in order to grasp how the Holy Spirit uses *joy* and its related words. Such a study would make it clear that joy and grace are intimately connected, as are the ideas of joy and the gifts of God. In other words, a study of the biblical meaning of joy drives us out of ourselves into our God. We will realize that joy is not rooted in us, our circumstances, our attainments, or our achievements. Rather it is rooted in our God and Saviour and in what He has done and is doing for us.

Joy then is the pleasure that a Christian takes or feels in all that he is and has, and in all that he ever will be or ever will have, in union with Christ. It is a pleasure that makes him glad and content in the Lord, even when his physical circumstances may cause him pain and misery. That is Christian joy.

How the Holy Spirit Produces Joy in Believers

Now our text shows us how the Holy Ghost produces this joy in believers. We read that joy is "the fruit of the Spirit." It is something that the Holy Ghost works in believers. Paul told the Thessalonians, "Ye became followers of us, and of the Lord, having received the word in much affliction, with joy of the Holy Ghost" (1 Thessalonians 1:6). The Holy Ghost is the author of Christian joy. It is He who works it in our hearts. Clearly He does so in two basic ways.

First, He witnesses to us of all we are and have in Christ. Witnessing is one of the great works of the Holy Spirit. He carries to the hearts of His people the assurance of the glad tidings of the gospel. He bears to our hearts the same message that the angels gave to the Judaean shepherds when they announced the birth of the Lord Jesus: "Behold, I bring you good tidings of great joy" (Luke 2:10). The work of the Spirit is to witness to us of things that produce joy. Paul terms this joy the "joy of faith" (Philippians 1:25) because it depends on our knowing and receiving the truth of the gospel. Perhaps this may help us grasp the reason for the lack of joy among professing Christians and the failure of most churches to alleviate the problem.

More than ever, churches produce programs to enhance the emotional health of their people. All too often they seek to brighten the mood of their people by the use of music, drama, or stories calculated to produce a given emotional response. Many even stoop to employing the gimmicks of a failed psychology. On the strength of such supposed helps to emotional welfare, churches send their people out to face the world, the flesh, and the devil. It is little wonder that the victims of such "help" end up more miserable than ever and are left bitter and frustrated. The reason is simple. In these cases the church is substituting sensual experience for spiritual joy. Spiritual joy comes only by an understanding and reception of the truth of the gospel.

We have seen that the Holy Ghost produces joy in us by witnessing to us of our position in Christ, our possessions in Christ, and our prospects in Christ. The joy that He imparts to us on this basis is real joy. It will never prove false or empty. It will never leave us disappointed. Unlike the happiness that is based on temporal things, it does not flatter to deceive. Some ancient historians say that the Persians had a particularly cruel practice when they conquered a territory. They selected the noblest slave they could find and dispatched the others to a quick and bloody death. They proclaimed the selected slave a king, clothing him in purple, wining and dining him, and filling his time with pleasure, music, and dancing. As from his throne he saw the others die, he must have been a happy man. What he did not know was that this treatment would last for only three days. At the end of the third day he was butchered. That is just like the happiness that sin and Satan hold out to men. It is short-lived and deceptive, the precursor of endless misery. The joy of the Lord is completely different. It never promises what it does not deliver. It is real, it is eternal, and it is produced by the Holy Spirit's showing us Christ and all that we are and have in Him.

The second way the Holy Spirit produces spiritual joy in us is by working in us to sanctify us and to conform us to Christ. Not only is the work of Christ on our behalf a source of spiritual joy, but so also is the work of the Holy Spirit within us. His convictions are a cause for rejoicing. Of course we do not usually associate conviction of sin with joy but with sadness. The realization that we have sinned certainly brings grief to our hearts, but it should cause us to rejoice as we realize that the Holy Spirit has not given us over to our lusts. He has not given us up. While we have failed our God, He is still working in us and with us, cutting away the lusts of our flesh. I would much rather have God speak to me to convict me of my sin than for Him not to speak at all. David's prayer is appropriate for us all: "Unto thee will I cry, O Lord my rock; be not silent to me: lest, if thou be silent to me, I become like them that go down into the pit" (Psalm 28:1). There is nothing we ought to fear more than the silence of God. While our sinning is not a cause for happiness, the Holy Spirit's conviction is a cause for rejoicing.

Every stirring of grace and of spiritual desire is a cause to rejoice. Christians often berate themselves unnecessarily. They desire much to glorify their Saviour but fall far short of their desires. Consequently, they often conclude that they may not be saved at all. But even the holiest of God's servants feel this failure to fulfil their spiritual desires. We all come up short. This is not an excuse for sin; it is simply a recognition of the fact that the greater our vision of the glory of God, the more we will feel how far short we fall. But instead of being entirely cast down by this, we should rejoice that the Holy Spirit has stirred us to long after Christ. Remember the old Puritan dictum, "The desire for grace is grace." The stirring of the soul after spiritual things is a work of the Spirit of God within us and this fact should cause us to rejoice.

Of course every victory over sin and every effectual entrance into the throne room of God in prayer is a cause to rejoice that the Holy Spirit is working in us. The struggle to overcome Satan and sin may be intense. The battle in the place of prayer may rage long and hard. But the Holy Spirit gives His people victory in these areas. He makes us victors, not victims, and so causes us to rejoice that however weak we are, however difficult our circumstances, He is working out His sanctifying purpose in our lives.

A Word of Encouragement

Now let us use our text as a word of encouragement. The Bible speaks of "the joy of the Lord" and of "the joy of [His] salvation." The meaning is clear: if we have the Lord, if we have received His salvation, we should have joy.

If the gospel is true, this is exactly what we would expect. God Himself is essentially and inherently joyful. He is absolutely glad and satisfied with all He is, all He says, and all He does. He has all blessedness in Himself (Romans 1:25; 9:5). Moreover, He rejoices over His people: "The Lord thy God in the midst of thee is mighty; he will save, he will rejoice over thee with joy; he will rest in his love, he will joy over thee with singing" (Zephaniah 3:17). The Lord rejoices over us because He has loved us, He has saved us, He has put us into Christ, He has clothed us in the righteousness of Christ. God rejoices in Himself and He rejoices in His people.

Now if our God is rejoicing in Himself and in what He has done for and in His people, it should be clear to us how we should rejoice. We should rejoice in the things that rejoice the heart of God. This joy is the birthright of every believer. The right to joy does not lie in our personality or in our circumstances. It resides in our God, in what He is, and in His work for us and in us.

This joy is a gift of power to lift us to victory over the works of the flesh. The works of the flesh—adultery, fornication, uncleanness, lasciviousness, idolatry, witchcraft, variance, emulations, wrath, strife, seditions, heresies, envyings, murder, drunkenness, revellings and such like—have no attraction for, or dominion over, one who is filled with the joy of the Lord. Nehemiah tells us, "The joy of the Lord is your strength" (Nehemiah 8:10). The joy of the Lord is more than a pleasant feeling; it is a mighty, spiritual principle of virtue that God places in the life of the believer. It enables us to cope with circumstances that otherwise would overcome us. It empowers us to conquer lusts that otherwise would consume us. The person who rejoices in the Lord will live in Christian victory, for joy is a gift of power.

What an encouragement this is! We do not have to work up the strength or produce certain character traits in order to overcome the world, the flesh, and the devil. The fruit of the Spirit—the natural result of knowing God in Christ—is the key to our victory. Our God is a rejoicing God, and He has given us the birthright of spiritual joy, a powerful gift that gives us the liberty and power to live the Christian life even when our physical circumstances and material conditions are not such as would make us happy.

A Word of Exhortation

We will finish this study with a word of exhortation. All that I have said should bring peace and consolation to believers. Yet I fear that it actually places a question mark over our Christian experience and the reality of the work of grace in our lives. Many believers reason, "Joy is the mark of a true believer; I fear that I have little or no real joy; therefore, I must not be a true believer." This sounds like good logic. Let us consider the matter carefully, however. Let us pose a question to any who reason in this fashion: "Is it really true that you take no pleasure in Christ?" If this is true of you, then it is clear that you are not a Christian. "If any man love not the Lord Jesus Christ, let him be Anathema Maranatha" (1 Corinthians 16:22). But is it really true that you have *no* pleasure in Christ?

If you do take pleasure in Christ, that is joy begun. It may be far from being perfected, but at least it is joy begun. The fruit is there, but it needs to be cultivated. The command of Scripture to cultivate it is given in Philippians 4:4: "Rejoice in the Lord alway: and again I say, Rejoice." James adjures us, "My brethren, count it all joy when ye fall into divers temptations [or trials]" (James 1:2). Both these Scriptures tell us that right thinking is the key to being able to rejoice in the face of the trials and sufferings of life. James uses the word *count*, which in other places is translated "think" and "esteem." It is a word that carries the connotation of ruling or governing. Thus James exhorts us to exercise rule over our trials by thinking rightly, remembering that they are "work[ing] for us a far more exceeding and eternal weight of glory" (2 Corinthians 4:17). The Philippians passage lists the things that should occupy our thoughts, things that will produce joy and peace: "Finally, brethren, whatsoever things are true, whatsoever things are honest, whatsoever things are just, whatsoever things are pure, whatsoever things are lovely, whatsoever things are of good report; if there be any virtue, and if there be any praise, think on these things" (Philippians 4:8).

The trouble with many Christians is that they think they should experience deep spiritual joy without much spiritual thought. They spend most of their time filling their minds with the thoughts and themes of the world and give very little time to the perusal of the great truths of the gospel. Is it any wonder, then, that in such people spiritual joy should be underdeveloped? If the Holy Spirit has planted His fruit in our hearts, we must cultivate it.

The apostle Peter provides us with a vivid example of precisely how we are to do this. He was writing to believers who were living in peril of their lives. They were experiencing a raging trial of their faith and were "in heaviness through manifold temptations" (1 Peter 1:6). That is, they had been put to grief by various trials. The word *heaviness* signifies a deep affliction or distress of mind. What sounds so incomprehensible is the immediate context of those words. Peter says, "Wherein ye greatly rejoice, though now for a season, if need be, ye are in heaviness."

We naturally ask how these people could be suffering deep distress of mind and rejoicing at the same time. The key to understanding this is in the word *wherein* ("Wherein ye greatly rejoice"). That word carries us back to the glorious statement of the gospel privileges Peter's readers enjoyed, privileges that were real whatever their current earthly situation. Mark them carefully, for it is by grasping these things that we too will experience a joy that nothing on earth can take from us.

Here are the things we rejoice in: "Elect according to the foreknowledge of God the Father, through sanctification of the Spirit, unto obedience and sprinkling of the blood of Jesus Christ: Grace unto you, and peace, be multiplied. Blessed be the God and Father of our Lord Jesus Christ, which according to his abundant mercy hath begotten us again unto a lively hope by the resurrection of Jesus Christ from the dead, to an inheritance incorruptible, and undefiled, and that fadeth not away, reserved in heaven for you, who are kept by the power of God through faith unto salvation ready to be revealed in the last time. Wherein ye greatly rejoice" (1 Peter 1:2–6).

What do we rejoice in? We rejoice that we are elect according to the foreknowledge, or predetermined counsel (Acts 2:23), of God the Father. We rejoice that He has chosen us as His people and has accordingly sanctified us by His Spirit unto the obedience of faith (not because of our foreseen faith). We rejoice that He has purified us by the sprinkling of the blood of Jesus Christ and has begotten us again to a lively hope by the resurrection of Jesus Christ from the dead. We rejoice that He guarantees us an inheritance that is incorruptible, undefiled, and unfading. We rejoice that not only has He reserved our inheritance in heaven for us, but He also stands guard over us by His power to bring us infallibly through faith to salvation ready to be revealed in the last time.

These are the things that we rejoice in. They are unchangeable. They stand true no matter what our earthly circumstances. Circumstances are very immediate and very demanding. Christian joy calls us to look beyond immediate circumstances to the great realities of the gospel. About four hundred years ago a martyr was slain in Rome. Before his death he lay in a terrible position, enduring terrible pain, in terrible surroundings, condemned to die. He addressed the last letter he wrote to friends outside the prison, "From the Pleasure Garden." These were his final words:

Who will believe that which I now state? In a dark hole I
have found cheerfulness; in a place of bitterness and death I
have found rest and the hope of salvation. Where others
weep I have found laughter; where others fear I have found
strength. Who will believe that in such a state of great misery I have had great pleasure; that in a lonely corner I have
had glorious company, and in the hardest bonds, perfect
repose? All these things Jesus my Saviour has granted me.
He is with me; He comforts me; He fills me with joy; He
drives bitterness from me, and gives me strength and
consolation.

That is joy, the fruit of the Spirit. Billy Sunday said, "If you have no
joy in your religion, there's a leak in your Christianity somewhere." That
leak may spring from a variety of causes. We may allow circumstances
to dominate our thinking and so obscure our joy. Even worse, at times
sin robs us of the joy of our salvation. When that happened to David, he
repented and prayed, "Restore unto me the joy of thy salvation" (Psalm
51:12). We should do the same.

Here is the exhortation. Is there is a leak in your Christianity? Then,
plug the leak. To change the metaphor, cultivate the fruit that the Holy
Ghost has begun to produce. Root out the weeds of wrong thinking and
wrong living. Get your eyes on Christ and on His "so great salvation":

- Look back to the covenant and the cross to find the cause of your joy.

- Look up to the throne where Christ is seated on the right hand of
  God for the confirmation of joy.

- Look forward to His coming for the crown of your joy.

Remember Thomas Watson's statement. May the God of all grace
grant that each of us may know that joy has begun to enter into us and
that we are on our way to heaven to enter into joy.

Peace that Passes Understanding

"The fruit of the Spirit is . . . peace."
Galatians 5:22

God is called "the God of peace" (1 Thessalonians 5:23). The gospel is by definition "the gospel of peace" (Romans 10:15). According to what Peter told Cornelius, peace is the very essence of the message that the Lord Jesus came to preach. He termed it "the word which God sent unto the children of Israel, preaching peace by Jesus Christ" (Acts 10:36). Peace formed a vital part of Christ's solemn promise to His disciples. Just before going to the cross He assured them, "Peace I leave with you, my peace give I unto you: not as the world giveth, give I unto you. Let not your heart be troubled, neither let it be afraid" (John 14:27). It is no wonder, therefore, that the word of God constantly assures God's people that there is peace for them in the midst of a troubled world, that God and His Son fully intend them to enjoy peace, that indeed peace is one of the marked blessings of being under the kingship of Christ. We read, "The kingdom of God is . . . righteousness, and peace, and joy in the Holy Ghost" (Romans 14:17). And we frequently see benedictions such as, "Grace be unto you and peace from God our Father and from the Lord Jesus Christ." Certainly it is clear that Christians should have peace in themselves and should be at peace with others, especially in the church. God's promise is that He will keep him in perfect peace whose mind is stayed on Him (Isaiah 26:3). He commands us, "Follow peace with all men" (Hebrews 12:14) and particularly, "be at peace among yourselves" (1 Thessalonians 5:13).

These simple truths lie on the surface of the word of God. They immediately present us with a problem of striking proportions, however. If God has provided peace for His people through the Lord Jesus Christ, if He has promised peace to them in every circumstance, how is it that so many of us distinctly lack a sense of peace? We may blame our circumstances. We may blame other people. Without doubt, circumstances and people may be very trying and may drive us to worry and fear. We should ask ourselves this question, however: "Is grace not stronger than our nature, our circumstances, and our sin?" If, as Paul states in Romans 5:20, grace is greater than all our sin, then it is greater than all that Satan and the world can throw at us. As a Christian grace, peace can grow in any climate, but the question remains: "Why do we lack peace?"

In answering this question we must remember that peace is "the fruit of the Spirit." That is, it is something the Holy Spirit produces because of His distinctive relationship to us and because of His peculiar work in us. Peace is produced in us by the present, powerful activity of the indwelling Spirit of God. It is His fruit. Once again we must emphasize a truth that we have considered in earlier chapters. We do not bear this fruit solely because we have been born again of the Spirit. That is essential, but we all know from experience that it is possible to be born of the Spirit and yet not to be currently experiencing the powerful working of His sanctifying power. This failure hinders the production of spiritual fruit in our lives. The works of the flesh inevitably blight the production of the fruit of Spirit, including the peace of the Spirit.

We may have, and indeed should have, this peace. It is natural for a Christian to enjoy it because it is the fruit the Holy Spirit's working. Paul's blessing on the Thessalonian believers is God's blessing on all His people: "The Lord of peace himself give you peace always by all means" (2 Thessalonians 3:16). We must consider some of the means by which the Holy Spirit produces the fruit of peace in His people.

The Peace of Assurance

The Holy Spirit produces the peace of God in us by giving us the assurance of salvation. Lack of assurance plagues many professing Christians, and indeed many true believers. All too often when believers who lack assurance seek help from pastors or counselors they are directed to a morbid introspection. There is a place for scriptural self-examination for, as we have noted, the indulgence of sin is the enemy of peace, particularly the peace of assurance. However, it is tragic when sincere souls plagued with lack of assurance are told to examine the character of their faith or of their decision, or the depth of their sincerity. It is destructive to tell such a person, as many have been told, "If you are not sure that your first decision for Christ was right, then put the matter beyond doubt by making another decision." The problem with this approach is that it produces only temporary relief. Before long the same old questions arise: "Did I pray the right prayer? Did I feel sufficient repentance? Did I really believe?" Where in the Bible does the Lord distinguish between believing and *really* believing? You either believe or you do not believe. This way of seeking assurance proceeds on the false idea that assurance may be had by detecting some adequate basis for it in what we have done. It is the notion that if only we can convince ourselves we have repented or believed to a certain degree of perfection, then we will have no reason to doubt our salvation. A moment's consideration should drive all such folly from our hearts. There is no genuine peace and assurance to be had in this way, only a Pharisaical presumption.

The Holy Spirit produces the peace of assurance in an entirely different manner. He gives us assurance by writing three great truths on our hearts. He assures us first that God is satisfied with what Christ has done on our behalf; second, that therefore we are justified freely by His grace, which is received by faith without any merit of our own; and third, that Christ is all-sufficient in His person and work as our Saviour. These truths are central to the gospel, and it is by bearing personal witness to them in the hearts of believers that the Holy Spirit fills believers with the peace of assurance. Thus the first thing the Holy Spirit does to give us the peace of assurance is to teach us the gospel of Jesus Christ. That is how we gain assurance.

God Is Satisfied

It is the constant witness of the Holy Spirit that all spiritual peace rests squarely on the merits of Christ's atonement. Apart from that we are enemies of God and under His wrath. Paul describes our life outside of Christ: "We were enemies" (Romans 5:10). As enemies, we were cut off from God and sunk in the darkness of sin. Paul sets forth the state of men apart from Christ: "Having the understanding darkened, being alienated from the life of God through the ignorance that is in them, because of the blindness of their heart" (Ephesians 4:18). As Isaiah says, "There is no peace, saith my God, to the wicked" (Isaiah

57:21). So long as we remained in sin we were under God's awful wrath. While we were His enemies we could have no peace.

The gospel provides the only answer to this wretched state. That answer centers on Christ as the sacrifice to satisfy the justice and law of God. He was our substitute who bore the wrath that was our due and so removed it from us forever. It is one of the most important truths of Scripture that Christ's atoning work is directed in the first place not toward man but toward God. Unless it is successful in its work toward God it can have no saving power toward man. According to Romans 3:25 the gospel is that "God hath set forth [Christ] to be a propitiation through faith in his blood." By the shedding of His precious blood the Lord Jesus Christ offered unto God a sacrifice that extinguishes the fire of the divine wrath of God against His people and lays the ground for their complete reconciliation and acceptance with God. As Paul put it, "It pleased the Father that in him should all fulness dwell; and, having made peace through the blood of his cross, by him to reconcile all things unto himself; . . . And you, that were sometime alienated and enemies in your mind by wicked works, yet now hath he reconciled" (Colossians 1:19–21). Here is the sure ground of the peace of assurance: God is satisfied. His wrath has been appeased. His law has been fulfilled and our account has been settled once and for all by the death of Christ.

Nothing is more conducive to peace of heart and mind than to know that God has nothing at all against you, not a sin unexpiated, not a debt unpaid. Christ has satisfied God and His law.

We Are Justified

Because God has been satisfied, we are justified. These two truths go together. Paul spells out this connection in Romans 3:24–25: "Being justified freely by his grace through the redemption that is in Christ Jesus: whom God hath set forth to be a propitiation through faith in his blood." Again he says that we have been "justified by his blood" (Romans 5:9). This is a wonderful truth, well calculated to impart the peace of assurance. It tells us that through the righteous merits of Christ we have received a complete pardon for all our sin and that we have also received the "gift of righteousness" (Romans 5:17), even the imputation of Christ's perfect obedience (Romans 5:18–19). Here is a sure way to enjoy peace. Grasping the truth of Isaiah's amazing description of justifying grace is key to gaining assurance with all the peace of conscience it brings: "I will greatly rejoice in the Lord, my soul shall be joyful in my God; for he hath clothed me with the garments of salvation, he hath covered me with the robe of righteousness" (Isaiah 61:10).

Christ Is All-Sufficient

It is clear that in convincing us that God is satisfied and that we are justified, the Holy Spirit bears witness that the merits of Christ are all-sufficient. Peace comes by Jesus Christ. Ephesians chapter 2 makes three important statements about the relation of our peace to the merits of Christ. First, He *is* our peace (verse 14). Second, He *made* peace (verse 15). Third, He came and *preached* peace (verse 17). Christ's preaching of peace depends on His making of peace. This is clear from every statement of Scripture about the finished, meritorious, and saving work of the Lord Jesus. For example, "This man, after he had offered one sacrifice for sins for ever, sat down on the right hand of God; . . . For by one offering he hath perfected for ever them that are sanctified" (Hebrews 10:12, 14). In Hebrews 10 sanctification refers not to the daily growth in grace of a believer but to his position of perfect acceptance in union with Christ and on the sole merit of Christ's atonement. In other words, He has perfected forever all His justified people. His merit is all-sufficient. It cannot fall short of complete success in achieving all that Christ aimed at in His life and death. Paul makes this point very clearly in Romans 8:30: "Whom he justified, them he also glorified." A sight of the all-sufficient merits of Christ, a conviction of the certain success of the Saviour in all He set out to accomplish by His obedience unto death is a sure way of gaining the peace of assurance. Augustus M. Toplady expressed this beautifully in his hymn "From Whence This Fear and Unbelief?":

> From whence this fear and unbelief?
> Hath not the Father put to grief
> His spotless Son for me?
> And will the righteous Judge of men
> Condemn me for that debt of sin
> Which, Lord, was charged on Thee?
>
> Complete atonement Thou hast made,
> And to the utmost Thou hast paid
> Whate'er Thy people owed;
> How then can wrath on me take place,
> If sheltered in Thy righteousness,
> And sprinkled with Thy blood?

If Thou hast my discharge procured,
And freely in my room endured
The whole of wrath divine;
Payment God cannot twice demand,
First at my bleeding Surety's hand,
And then again at mine.

Turn then my soul unto thy rest!
The merits of thy great High Priest
Have bought thy liberty;
Trust in His efficacious blood,
Nor fear thy banishment from God,
Since Jesus died for thee.

Here then is how the Holy Spirit gives His people the assurance of salvation. That assurance depends on a clear sight by faith of our all-sufficient Saviour. It is by exhibiting Him to our hearts and minds that the Spirit gives us peace. Thus the Scriptures constantly present Christ as the object of our faith. This is a vital truth. The perfection of faith is not in our exercise of it but in its object, namely the person and work of Christ:

- *Faith in Christ crucified* yields the peace of knowing that "there is therefore now no condemnation to them that are in Christ Jesus" (Romans 8:1).

- *Faith in Christ risen and ascended* yields the peace of confidence that our Saviour has obtained all the gifts and graces we need to serve Him : "When he ascended up on high, he led captivity captive, and gave gifts unto men" (Ephesians 4:8). Included in the gift of the risen Christ is the confidence that we can overcome Satan and all his powers. As Paul assured the believers at Rome, "The God of peace shall bruise Satan under your feet shortly" (Romans 16:20).

- *Faith in Christ returning* yields the peace of certain hope. His return is "the blessed hope" of His people (Titus 2:13), in the light of which we live pure lives (1 John 3:3), knowing that whatever the future holds for us it is inevitably leading to the return of our great God and Saviour, Jesus Christ. Thus we live in the peace of that hope: "The God of hope fill you with all joy and peace in believing,

  that ye may abound in hope, through the power of the Holy Ghost" (Romans 15:13).

Thus the Holy Spirit's first action in producing the fruit of peace in His people is to give them the assurance of salvation. Convinced by the Spirit that they have peace with God—that is, that they are reconciled to Him because they have been justified by grace through faith in Christ's all-sufficient merits—believers are equipped to live as victors over their immediate circumstances and not as victims of them.

Peace Through Prayer

The Holy Spirit also gives us peace of mind by teaching us the power of prayer. Worry is a great enemy of faith and prayer. Consumed by anxiety, we cannot conquer by prayer. The plain command of our Saviour is, "Take no thought for your life, what ye shall eat, or what ye shall drink; nor yet for your body, what ye shall put on" (Matthew 6:25). "Take no thought" means simply "be not anxious," "be not full of care." Our Lord repeats His admonition a few verses later, "Take therefore no thought for the morrow: for the morrow shall take thought for the things of itself" (verse 34). Paul uses the same word in advising the Philippian Christians and goes on to spell out for them how to live in peace instead of being weighed down by anxious care: "Be careful for nothing; but in every thing by prayer and supplication with thanksgiving let your requests be made known unto God. And the peace of God, which passeth all understanding, shall keep your hearts and minds through Christ Jesus" (Philippians 4:6-7).

Usually the advice not to worry is fatuous and futile. For us to tell someone not to worry is a way of insuring that he does not bother us with what is worrying him, for we have no way of removing the cause of his anxiety. However, when Paul says, "Do not worry," he at once goes on to show how to fulfill the command. He gives the alternative to worry: thank God for all He has done for you and place your present needs before Him. The result will be that "the peace of God will keep [stand guard over] your hearts and minds." How does this protection of the mind occur? The apostle gives a clear answer in verses 8–9: "Finally, brethren, whatsoever things are true, whatsoever things are honest, whatsoever things are just, whatsoever things are pure, whatsoever things are lovely, whatsoever things are of good report; if there be any virtue, and if there be any praise, think on these things. Those things, which ye have both learned, and received, and heard, and seen in me, do: and the God of peace shall be with you."

Here Paul shows the vital importance of being able to think clearly about the truths of the gospel. All the things that he says should occupy our minds have their highest expression in Christ and His gospel. Thus he is teaching us to look at everything through the truth of the gospel, to interpret everything in the light of the triple truth we have considered: God is satisfied; I am justified; Christ is all-sufficient. In the light of this truth we should consider any situation and give thanks to God. There is always a reason to praise Him. If I am sick, I may not enjoy the experience but I can praise God that I am not in hell. I *could* be there, and if I were to receive even a fraction of what I deserve, I *would* be there, but by God's grace I am not and never will be. If the sickness kills me, I am going to heaven, and surely that is a matter for great thanksgiving. This does not mean that we should not take prudent action to deal with our physical ailments. What it does mean is that we should remember that we have much to be thankful for. We should not question God's love because of current circumstances. Neither should we give in to debilitating anxiety. We should rather think on the glorious truths of the gospel and in their light worship and pray. When we do, three things will happen. First, we will be able to face our troubles. Second, the peace of God will stand guard over our hearts and minds. Third, the God of peace Himself will lighten our darkness with His presence.

When the Holy Spirit teaches us the power of prayer, He not only gives us the ability to obtain divine answers to our problems and divine provisions for our needs, He places in our hands the key to enjoying peace of mind.

Peace Through Trusting God's Sovereignty

The Holy Spirit gives us peace of mind amidst all the troubles of life by reminding us of the sovereignty of our Father in heaven. He witnesses to us of "the purpose of Him who worketh all things after the counsel of His own will" (Ephesians 1:11). It is easy for most of us to feel a sense of peace and wellbeing when things are going as we wish. But when dark clouds of adversity roll in it is often a different story. We question why God would allow such things to happen and so lose our peace. The truth is that our God is in complete control. He is neither worried by what is happening nor surprised by it. He has laid down His purpose from all eternity and He is working it out according to His plan. Nothing can overthrow His purpose, for "His kingdom ruleth over all" (Psalm 103:19). Though we cannot understand the secret counsel of God (Deuteronomy 29:29), when we enter His presence in prayer we should never forget the truth of Jeremiah 17:12: "A glorious high throne from the beginning is the place of our sanctuary." Our Father does all things well, even those things that perplex us. We must learn that He warns us, as Christ did His disciples, "What I do thou knowest not now; but thou shalt know hereafter" (John 13:7). Meanwhile, the assurance of the all-wise sovereignty of God our Father is a fruitful ground of peace of mind.

Job knew something of this when he lost wealth, family, and health. His wife was overcome with bitterness, but Job replied, "What? shall we receive good at the hand of God, and shall we not receive evil [calamity]?" (Job 2:10). He knew that his circumstances had not robbed God of His sovereignty and he trusted that God's sovereignty was right and good. This is the confidence believers have in Christ: "We know that all things work together for good to them that love God, to them who are the called according to his purpose" (Romans 8:28). We may not be able to trace the steps by which all things are working together for our good, but our God can. Our trust in His all-wise sovereignty delivers us from needless anxiety and bitterness.

At times we may feel as Jacob did. Having lost Joseph and Simeon and being threatened with the loss of Benjamin, he cried, "All these things are against me" (Genesis 42:36). In fact, just as he was lamenting his ill fortune, God was working out the details of his reunion with Joseph. He was going to lose nothing, but at the moment he could see no further than his grief. When we are blinded by grief or worry, or by anything else, so that we lose sight of the sovereignty of our God, we throw away our peace. When we rest on the infallible truth that He is working all things for His own glory and for the ultimate good of His people, we will enjoy peace. Let us never forget that we have a gracious Father in heaven and trust all to His wise disposition, remembering Peter's advice to cast "all your care upon him; for he careth for you" (1 Peter 5:7).

Some years ago a Christian family was enjoying a quiet drive in their automobile. A drunken driver suddenly smashed into them. Their little daughter was thrown through the windshield and landed on the side of the road. She was killed instantly. Naturally father and mother were shocked and broken-hearted. Nevertheless, that young mother cradled her little daughter's dead body in her arms and lifted her eyes to heaven, quoting the words of Job, "The Lord gave, and the Lord hath taken away; blessed be the name of the Lord" (Job 1:21). She found peace in accepting the sovereignty of God, even when the immediate source of her trouble was the wicked actions of a drunkard. The only alternative would have been to become bitter, angry, fretful, and distracted—all of which would have worsened her loss. The more we fret, struggle, or become angry, frustrated, and bitter, the less peace we will have. If only we can fix our attention on the greatness of our God and trust Him who created all things and who sustains all things to do what is wise and good, we will have peace amid all the troubles of life. This is more than theory. It is what the Lord Himself taught Job as He reasoned with him about his reaction to his troubles. In the closing chapters of the book of Job, the Lord does not explain anything of His secret purpose in permitting Satan to attack Job. Rather He gave Job a vision of His own greatness and sovereignty and that was enough to restore Job to perfect peace of mind—even before the pain of his trials had been removed.

Peace in the Valley

The Holy Spirit gives us peace when facing death by giving us the knowledge of the presence of Christ and the assurance of a place in heaven. Jesus said, "Let not your heart be troubled: ye believe in God, believe also in me. In my Father's house are many mansions: if it were not so, I would have told you. I go to prepare a place for you. And if I go and prepare a place for you, I will come again, and receive you unto myself; that where I am, there ye may be also" (John 14:1–3). Nothing imparts a well-grounded peace to the dying more than the experience of the presence of the Lord with them and His assurance that He is taking them home to heaven. This was David's assurance: "Yea, though I walk through the valley of the shadow of death, I will fear no evil: for thou art with me; thy rod and thy staff they comfort me" (Psalm 23:4). We like to think that when we face death we will have our loved ones around us. That is natural, but it is far more important to have our Saviour there, and He promises that He will not fail to be present in that hour.

To be able to face death in the calm assurance that it is well with our souls and that we will soon be in heaven is peace indeed. And it is the privilege of every believer: "For we know that if our earthly house of this tabernacle were dissolved, we have a building of God, an house not made with hands, eternal in the heavens. . . . We are confident, I say, and willing rather to be absent from the body, and to be present with the Lord" (2 Corinthians 5:1, 8). We can say with Paul, "I know whom I have believed, and am persuaded that he is able to keep that which I have committed unto him against that day" (2 Timothy 1:12).

That is how I want to die. That is the assurance, the peace, I want to experience. The Holy Spirit promises to impart that peace by giving the assurance of the presence of Christ and the certainty of a place in heaven on His merits. In the light of this assurance we who know Christ may enjoy the fullness of His promise: "Peace I leave with you, my peace I give unto you: not as the world giveth, give I unto you. Let not your heart be troubled, neither let it be afraid" (John 14:27).

The Peace of Christian Unity

Thus far we have considered the subject of peace in terms of personal experience, but it also has a corporate aspect. The Holy Spirit grants us the peace of unity in the church by teaching Christians their place in the body of Christ. The command of God to Christians in regard to unity is plain and repeated often in Scripture. The following texts are typical of the urgent calls for peace and unity in Christ's church:

> Ephesians 4:1–3: "I therefore, the prisoner of the Lord, beseech you that ye walk worthy of the vocation wherewith ye are called, with all lowliness and meekness, with longsuffering, forbearing one another in love; endeavouring to keep the unity of the Spirit in the bond of peace."

> Philippians 1:27; 2:2; 3:16: "Stand fast in one spirit, with one mind striving together for the faith of the gospel. . . . Fulfil ye my joy, that ye be likeminded, having the same love, being of one accord, of one mind. . . . Let us walk by the same rule, let us mind the same thing."

> Romans 15:5–6: "The God of patience and consolation grant you to be likeminded one toward another according to Christ Jesus: that ye may with one mind and one mouth glorify God, even the Father of our Lord Jesus Christ."

> 1 Corinthians 14:33: "God is not the author of confusion, but of peace, as in all churches of the saints."

1 Thessalonians 5:13: "Be at peace among yourselves."

This unity among God's people is a great boon and is productive of great good. David describes its results in Psalm 133: "Behold, how good and how pleasant it is for brethren to dwell together in unity! It is like the precious ointment upon the head, that ran down upon the beard, even Aaron's beard: that went down to the skirts of his garments; as the dew of Hermon, and as the dew that descended upon the mountains of Zion: for there the Lord commanded the blessing, even life for evermore."

The fact that brotherly unity is attended by such blessing places a heavy burden of responsibility on us to do nothing to injure or destroy it. Anything that costs the church the anointing of divine power or the dew of heaven's blessing is indefensible. Sinful divisions—schisms, the pursuit of selfish or sectional interests—exact a terrible price. They drive away the gracious Holy Spirit and so rob us of His refreshing presence and power. Unity is not an option, it is a necessity.

There is such a thing as biblical separation. Christians should "have no fellowship with the unfruitful works of darkness, but rather reprove them" (Ephesians 5:11). The unity of the Christian church is not an amalgamation of belief and unbelief, of orthodoxy and heterodoxy. On this issue the Bible is clear: "Be ye not unequally yoked together with unbelievers: for what fellowship hath righteousness with unrighteousness? and what communion hath light with darkness? And what concord hath Christ with Belial? or what part hath he that believeth with an infidel? And what agreement hath the temple of God with idols? for ye are the temple of the living God; as God hath said, I will dwell in them, and walk in them; and I will be their God, and they shall be my people. Wherefore come out from among them, and be ye separate, saith the Lord, and touch not the unclean thing; and I will receive you, And will be a Father unto you, and ye shall be my sons and daughters, saith the Lord Almighty" (2 Corinthians 6:14–18). Paul commands us to turn away from those who do not maintain faith in the teachings of Christ (1 Timothy 6:3–5). Separation is an aspect of holiness, and always has Christ as its focus: "Wherefore Jesus also, that he might sanctify the people with his own blood, suffered without the gate. Let us go forth therefore unto him without the camp, bearing his reproach" (Hebrews 13:13).

Separation is therefore entirely different from needless division, which is always an aspect of carnality. Where there is a sincere adherence to the great doctrinal truths of the word of God and a humble submission to the full and final authority of Scripture in all matters of faith and practice, we should lay aside all petty, personal differences and "keep the unity of the Spirit in the bond of peace" (Ephesians 4:3). This is every Christian's responsibility, but it will be fulfilled by the grace of God as His Spirit works among His people. We read that in the days of Hezekiah, when the king called all Israel to Jerusalem to renew their covenant with the Lord, "in Judah the hand of God was to give them one heart to do the commandment of the king and of the princes, by the word of the Lord" (2 Chronicles 30:12). Unity is a divine gift and grace.

The Holy Spirit exercises this grace among His people by teaching them the beautiful truth that the church is the body of Christ and that each believer is a particular member of that body. In the diversity of the many members there is a central unity, so that each Christian must fulfill his God-given function in the body. Paul combated the divisions that rent the Corinthian church by emphasizing this truth:

> As the body is one, and hath many members, and all the members of that one body, being many, are one body: so also is Christ. For by one Spirit are we all baptized into one body, whether we be Jews or Gentiles, whether we be bond or free; and have been all made to drink into one Spirit. For the body is not one member, but many. If the foot shall say, Because I am not the hand, I am not of the body; is it therefore not of the body? And if the ear shall say, Because I am not the eye, I am not of the body; is it therefore not of the body? If the whole body were an eye, where were the hearing? If the whole were hearing, where were the smelling? But now hath God set the members every one of them in the body, as it hath pleased him. And if they were all one member, where were the body? But now are they many members, yet but one body. (1 Corinthians 12:12–20)

What a lovely picture this presents of a church using all the diverse abilities and gifts of all its members to the glory of their common head, the Lord Jesus Christ! God's people, called together to serve in the fellowship of the gospel, are instructed to lay aside all ego and self-promotion. These have no place in the body of Christ, where all our energies must be on promoting Christ. As we see ourselves not as so many individuals with rights to protect and axes to grind but as members of Christ's body, we will enjoy the blessing of the fruit of the Spirit, which is peace. And we will have the blessed experience Paul described to the Ephesians: Christ is the head "from whom the whole body fitly joined together and compacted [or, 'knit together'] by that which every joint supplieth, according to the effectual working in the measure of every part [or, 'according to the effective working by which every part does its share'], maketh increase of [or, 'causes growth in'] the body unto the edifying of itself in love" (Ephesians 4:16).

There is a full harvest of peace, the fruit of the Spirit, for believers to experience in their personal lives and in the life of the church. May "the Lord of peace himself give you peace always by all means."

Patience Under Pressure

"The fruit of the Spirit is . . . longsuffering."
Galatians 5:22

Nine graces constitute the fruit of the Spirit. Each of them affects every part of the believer's life. Each influences all the upward motions of the soul to govern the believer's dealings with God. Each influences all the outward motions of his soul to govern his dealings with others. Each influences the inward motions of his soul to govern his attitudes and actions toward himself.

Yet, as we have noted in our earlier study, these nine graces fall into three groups of three. The first three—love, joy, and peace—are mainly exercised with respect to God. They emphasize our relationship with Him. The second three—longsuffering, gentleness, and goodness—are mainly exercised toward other people. The final three—faith, meekness, and temperance—are chiefly directed inward. They describe what we are in ourselves. In this chapter we commence our investigation into the second group of three: longsuffering, gentleness, and goodness.

One of the marks of the Holy Spirit's work in believers is His production of a Christlike spirit in our dealings with other people. A man whose religion does not radically affect his attitude and behavior toward other people probably has no saving knowledge of Christ at all. He cannot claim a right relationship with God if he has nothing of the likeness of Christ about the way he treats his fellow men. It is impossible for a man to know the love of God in his heart, to experience the joy of salvation filling his soul, and to have the peace of God ruling in his heart without these graces having a powerful influence over his attitudes and actions toward the people around him.

Longsuffering, gentleness, and *goodness* are the three words that would most likely spring to mind if we were asked to sum up the attitude and actions of the Lord Jesus Christ toward other people. If the work of the Spirit in sanctification is the fulfillment of God's predestinating purpose for us "to be conformed to the image of his Son" (Romans 8:29), then these same words should also describe us as we deal with others.

These three words are actually very close to one another in meaning and are therefore not easy to distinguish. Perhaps the simplest way of differentiating among them is as follows: The Greek term *makrothumia,* "longsuffering," emphasizes a Christlike temperament. The word *chrestotes,* "gentleness," denotes kindness and emphasizes a Christlike tenderness. The third word of the group, *agathosune,* "goodness," to all intents and purposes has the same meaning as *chrestotes.* Even eminent linguists are at a loss as to how exactly to distinguish between *gentleness* (or "kindness") and *goodness.* Their best suggestion is that if we understand gentleness as tenderness of heart, goodness is that tenderness in action. It emphasizes not merely kind feelings or thoughts but kind actions. So the third term teaches us to be Christlike in our treatment of others. Here is our calling as we walk among men. We are to carry ourselves before them in a Christlike manner. We are to be like our Master in temperament (or, temper, as we usually say), in tenderness, and in our treatment of other people.

Today slick marketers fill Christian bookstores with WWJD paraphernalia—What would Jesus do? That is the theme of a fictional book that falls far short of an evangelical understanding of the gospel. The question, What would Jesus do? is usually answered according to the current notions of political correctness. For the most part people do not answer the question of what Jesus would do from what the Scriptures say He did, but from what their own moral, social, and political prejudices have conditioned them to believe. So, as the question has been skillfully marketed to the modern church, WWJD is more often than not an excuse for unscriptural compromises that ignore the plain teachings of God's word. However, if we take the Bible as our textbook and the gospel as our foundation, blood-washed Christians will not go wrong in seeking to discover, "What would Jesus do?" Indeed, we should inquire, "What *did* Jesus do?" and seek to conform our lives to His image.

In this study we will examine the first term that describes our likeness to Christ in His dealings with others. "The fruit of the Spirit is . . . longsuffering." The central message of this study is easy to understand: Longsuffering is the work of the Holy Spirit in a believer to make him patient so that he will not be easily or quickly provoked to passion or intemperate action, especially to anger.

In pursuing this theme we must first carefully define the term *longsuffering*. Then we must see how the Holy Spirit produces this grace in a believer. Finally, we must personally apply what we learn and examine ourselves.

Longsuffering: What It Means

First, we must define the term longsuffering. The Greek word *makrothumia* simply means "long temper." In English we do not use the term long temper, though we are all familiar with short temper. A long temper is just the opposite of a short temper. The fruit of the Spirit is a long temper. The word describes a person who is not given to sudden, blazing anger. It is difficult to convey this with a single English word. *Longsuffering* may be the best we can do to convey the meaning of *makrothumia,* but it is not really the precise term we would desire. The proper word would be *longanimity,* if there were such a word. The Rheims translation of the Galatians 5:22 tried to introduce this word into our English vocabulary, but it did not catch on. In some ways this is strange because the word *magnanimity* became a popular English word to describe a big-hearted, generous attitude.

So, without such a word as *longanimity* we are left with *longsuffering.* The *suffering* part of the word refers to patience, so that longsuffering is the maintenance of a patient temperament under various kinds of provocation. Archbishop Trench, whose work on the synonyms of the New Testament is still the standard work on the subject, says that longsuffering means a long holding out of the mind before it gives room to passion or action, generally to passion. Evidently it is an aspect of patience. The word that is usually translated "patience" (*hupomone*) signifies "an abiding under" and describes the Christian humbly enduring difficult circumstances. Under the pressure of circumstances or things, he manifests a humble submission to God, remaining under the pressure without losing his faith and joy in the Lord. The word *longsuffering,* by contrast, denotes patience with regard to people rather than to things. It particularly describes patience under the provocation of difficult or injurious people. John Chrysostom, the golden-mouthed preacher of Constantinople and a disciple of John the apostle, added the idea of forbearance toward people who are provoking us, especially when we have the means and the opportunity to take vengeance upon them. The apostle Paul gives us a divine definition of longsuffering in Ephesians 4:1–2: "I therefore, the prisoner of the Lord, beseech you that ye walk worthy of the vocation wherewith ye are called, with all lowliness and meekness, with longsuffering, forbearing one another in love." *Forbearing one another in love.* That is precisely the force of the term.

According to our text longsuffering is a fruit of the Spirit. In other words, it is a Christian grace, what John Brown the Scottish theologian called, "a disposition and a habit" that grows out of the Holy Spirit's indwelling of, and continuing operation in, a believer. It is the usual state of mind and heart that the Spirit of God produces in those in whom He dwells and whom He is sanctifying into conformity to Christ. Thus, longsuffering is a grace. It is not a description of a natural disposition. We all know some people who are better natured than others. You have heard it said of someone, "He is very good natured." We may describe a person as "laid back." Sometimes this attitude arises from lassitude, disinterest, or timidity. What Paul is saying in Galatians is that all Christians, whatever our natural disposition, should be longsuffering because of the concerns that the Holy Spirit is working in our hearts.

It is the consistent testimony of Scripture that God calls His people to manifest this grace:

> Colossians 1:10-11: "Walk worthy of the Lord unto all pleasing, being fruitful in every good work, and increasing in the knowledge of God; strengthened with all might, according to his glorious power, unto all patience and longsuffering with joyfulness." You cannot walk worthy of the Lord unless you are walking with longsuffering.

> Colossians 3:12: "Put on therefore, as the elect of God, holy and beloved, bowels of mercies, kindness, humbleness of mind, meekness, longsuffering."

Hebrews 6:12: "Be not slothful, but followers of them who through faith and patience [Greek, *makrothumia*] inherit the promises."

James 5:10: "Take, my brethren, the prophets, who have spoken in the name of the Lord, for an example of suffering affliction, and of patience [Greek, *makrothumia*]."

The Lord highly prizes this virtue. He "is longsuffering to us-ward" (2 Peter 3:9) and pronounces His blessing on all who are "followers [or, 'imitators'] of God" (Ephesians 5:1) in this regard. He also denounces those who fail to exercise this virtue:

Proverbs 14:29: "He that is slow to wrath is of great understanding: but he that is hasty of spirit exalteth folly."

Proverbs 15:18: "A wrathful man stirreth up strife: but he that is slow to anger appeaseth strife."

Proverbs 16:32: "He that is slow to anger is better than the mighty; and he that ruleth his spirit than he that taketh a city."

Proverbs 25:28: "He that hath no rule over his own spirit is like a city that is broken down, and without walls."

The man who is always ready to flare up in anger and who has no control over his own spirit is not only a man without understanding, exalting folly and stirring up strife, he is a man who casts aside every defense against sin and Satan. He needs the fruit of the Spirit to enable him to conquer in the toughest battles of life, for the greatest conquerors in history are those who by the grace of God have conquered themselves. Mrs. A. A. Whiddington's hymn "Not I, but Christ" reflects this need in the prayer voiced in the refrain: "Oh, to be saved from myself, dear Lord." Salvation is more than deliverance from external evils such as alcohol and drugs. It is also a deliverance from internal dispositions toward self, from the tyranny of the inclinations of the flesh. It enables a Christian to rule his own spirit.

God places immense importance on this grace of longsuffering. It is necessary that we should grasp its meaning so that we may proceed to study and experience the actual production of this fruit in our lives.

Longsuffering: How the Spirit Produces It

We now we come to the heart of our subject—how the Holy Spirit produces longsuffering in His people. We will set out three distinct steps in this divine operation.

Conviction of Short Temper

The first thing the Holy Spirit does to bring us to the grace of being long tempered is to convict us of being short tempered. He makes us feel the wickedness of our short temper, our blowing up at sudden or slight provocation.

Short temper is sin. Let us make no excuse for it. It is sin for a Christian not to take time to weigh up the situation that is developing before him, to consider the feelings of other parties involved in it, and to seek the glory of God through it. To plunge into words or action without due consideration is sin. Christianity is a thinking religion. The gospel demands that we think, not simply react. We are called to apply the gospel to every situation, to step back from the immediate provocation and fix the immutable truth of the gospel in our minds, and thereby to respond in a godly manner. That is how we are supposed to live. That is what Paul means by living by faith—allowing what we believe to govern how we act. The only alternative to living like this is to give free expression to all that is selfish in us. It is utterly selfish to demand that we may give free rein to our feelings even though they may be only surface deep, to think that we must have the relief of getting things off our chest no matter what damage we may cause to others in doing so. Such selfishness is sin and greatly dishonors God.

Thus, it is a major work of the Holy Spirit to convict us of the sin of indulging our short temper. We have various ways of excusing our short temper, though we rarely extend the luxury of making such excuses to others. We say, "I have a short fuse." Or, "I am very intense and tend to blow up suddenly, but I do not hold a grudge." This self-serving excuse takes the cake! How kind! The person who turns the blowtorch of searing anger on another has the audacity to say to him, while he is still stinging from the attack, "Don't worry, I do not hold a grudge." Such excuses are unworthy of a Christian. He knows it, for the Holy Spirit convicts him of the wickedness of his ill temper.

Every one of us needs the Spirit's conviction and His work to produce the fruit of a long temper. His conviction may not make us feel good at the time and it may lead us into the depths of humiliation as we have to confess and apologize for our short temper, but it shows us that there is hope and help for us. When He identifies sin in our lives He is in reality giving us good news. By exposing sin He tells us that it is something for which we know the answer. We know what to do with sin. The worst news that anyone can give a person is to tell him that his problem is "just your personality," or that it is all in his genes. That is just another way of saying that there is no answer to the problem. According to the gospel, there is a way to deal with sin, including the sin of short temper. When the Holy Spirit convicts us of this sin He witnesses that by confessing our sin and submitting to His control "we may be strengthened with all might, according to his glorious power, unto all patience and long-suffering with joyfulness."

A Sight of God's Longsuffering

The Holy Spirit's second way of producing in us the fruit of long-suffering is by reminding us that God suffers long with sinners, including us, who provoke Him. We "provoked the Holy One of Israel unto anger" (Isaiah 1:4). The Old Testament is replete with references to Israel's provocation of the Lord. Deuteronomy 9:7 may be taken as representative of them: "Remember, and forget not, how thou provokedst the Lord thy God to wrath in the wilderness: from the day that thou didst depart out of the land of Egypt, until ye came unto this place, ye have been rebellious against the Lord." We are no better than they were. We have provoked Him, but "God is slow to anger." The Old Testament repeats this message many times:

> Nehemiah 9:17: "Thou art a God ready to pardon, gracious and merciful, slow to anger, and of great kindness."
>
> Psalm 103:8: "The Lord is merciful and gracious, slow to anger, and plenteous in mercy."
>
> Psalm 145:8: The Lord is gracious, and full of compassion; slow to anger, and of great mercy."
>
> Jonah 4:2: "[Jonah prayed to the Lord:] I knew that thou art a gracious God, and merciful, slow to anger, and of great kindness."
>
> Nahum 1:3: "The Lord is slow to anger, and great in power, and will not at all acquit the wicked."

The New Testament says the same thing:

> Romans 2:4: "Despisest thou the riches of his goodness and forbearance and longsuffering; not knowing that the goodness of God leadeth thee to repentance?"

> Romans 9:22: "What if God, willing to shew his wrath, and to make his power known, endured with much longsuffering the vessels of wrath fitted to destruction?"

> 1 Peter 3:20: "The longsuffering of God waited in the days of Noah, while the ark was a preparing."

> 2 Peter 3:15: "Account that the longsuffering of our Lord is salvation; even as our beloved brother Paul also according to the wisdom given unto him hath written unto you."

The message in all these texts is plain. God is longsuffering, even under the worst kind of provocation from us. As we have seen from Ephesians 5:1, Christians are to be imitators of God, and this includes being like Him in his longsuffering toward provoking people. Since longsuffering is the "fruit of the Spirit," it falls under the command of 1 Peter 1:16, "Be ye holy; for I am holy." It forms the rationale for the appeal that the apostle John makes, "Beloved, if God so loved us, we ought also to love one another" (1 John 4:11).

It is remarkable that worshipers become like the object of their worship. This is true of the heathen: "They that make them [idols] are like unto them; so is every one that trusteth in them" (Psalm 115:8). It is also true of Christians: "We all, with open face beholding as in a glass the glory of the Lord, are changed into the same image from glory to glory, even as by the Spirit of the Lord" (2 Corinthians 3:18). Thus, by impressing us with the longsuffering of our great God and Saviour, the Holy Spirit is taking decisive action to conform us to His image and produce that precious fruit in our lives.

Cultivation of Graces that Produce Longsuffering

The third way in which the Holy Spirit produces the fruit of patience under provocation is by enabling us to bring forth the graces on which it is based. The position of longsuffering in the list of virtues that constitute the fruit of the Spirit is instructive. It does not head the list, but comes after love, joy, and peace. The implication is clear: as long as we are right with God we will be right—and patient—with men. The person who enjoys the love of God and loves God in return, who is living in the joy of salvation, and who is experiencing the peace of a believing assurance in Christ will not live under the kind of intense pressure, frustration, anger, and selfishness that produce short temper.

Thus, a believer who is constantly flaring up and lashing out in rage needs to stop and think very seriously. He needs to ask himself, Why am I angry? That is the question that the Lord forced Jonah to face: "Doest thou well to be angry?" (Jonah 4:9). Is it becoming of a Christian who has peace with God and in whom the peace of God is supposed to rule and govern, to live with bitterness and anger? So short-tempered Christians should make themselves address the question, Why? They may particularly ask themselves, Why am I frustrated? Frustration is a frequent cause of short temper. Feeling that they have not achieved what they intended or that they have not been as successful as they hoped to have been, many Christians sink into the bitterness of frustration. It shows in their angry reactions to real or imagined provocations and they, for a time at least, behave as if God had not blessed them with all spiritual blessings in heavenly places in Christ (Ephesians 1:3). Instead of focusing on all the things they do not have or cannot do, Christians should count the blessings of grace. If they will seriously consider that God is their Father, Christ is their redeemer who has washed their sins away in His own blood, the Spirit is their comforter, the Bible is their charter and warrant of faith, and heaven is their home, they will be delivered from frustration that robs them of being patient under pressure.

This loss of patience under pressure does not arise by accident. Christians allow it to happen. By failing to lay hold of the provision God has made in Christ, they allow the pressure or the provocations they face to steal away their peace. Those who are living at peace with God and with themselves will live at peace with others. The man who lives on a short fuse is not at peace with himself and he is not living in the experience of the peace of God. The promise of God's word is unambiguous: "Be careful for nothing; but in every thing by prayer and supplication with thanksgiving let your requests be made known unto God. And the peace of God, which passeth all understanding, shall keep your hearts and minds through Christ Jesus" (Philippians 4:6–7).

This is a case where the more we live in the atmosphere of heaven, the more we will not allow the sudden or slight provocations from people to drive us to rage or to precipitate or intemperate action. What we say and do should be well thought out and tempered by the gospel. This means that we think so highly of the gospel, aim so single-mindedly at the glory of God, and enjoy so fully our fellowship with God that we refuse to allow the foolishness or the wickedness of other people to embitter our souls even for a short time.

Longsuffering: Do We Exhibit It?

In the light of all we have learned we must examine ourselves. Each one of us must ask himself some penetrating questions.

Has the longsuffering of God led me to repentance? Is my angry, bitter spirit the evidence of a heart that has never known faith and repentance? It is useless for any man to seek the fruit of the Spirit in his life until he is saved. All too often people who are euphemistically termed "carnal Christians" are quite simply people who have never been saved. I must first of all make my calling and election sure, as Peter admonishes (2 Peter 1:10).

If I am sure I am saved, I must ask the question, Is my temper destroying my testimony? It is foolish to imagine that I can be a wit-ness for Christ if I am so unlike Him as to be of a bitter, ill-tempered spirit.

Am I living in the power of the gospel? Is it governing how I think, act, and react? Does the truth of the gospel govern my temper? Or am I living an utterly selfish life, demanding that everyone and everything be as pleases me and reacting with violent or sullen anger if they are not? This is the mark of the short-tempered (or bad-tempered) man. If this is true of me, I am not living under the power of the gospel, but under the control of self.

Another important question is, How well do I imitate my Lord? To what extent have I been "changed into [His] image from glory to glory"? Do I consciously seek to be a fair reflection of Christ in my dealings with others?

How well does my attitude to others reflect the Lord's dealings with me? If the Lord were to deal with me as I deal with other people what would the result be? The command of God is clear: "Be ye kind one to another, tenderhearted, forgiving one another, even as God for Christ's sake hath forgiven you" (Ephesians 4:32). Do I take this so seriously that it governs my attitudes and actions toward others?

These are penetrating questions. We all need to ponder them long and hard. As we do, the Lord will show us what He expects as the norm for His people. We are not speaking about some super-Christianity, something for a small elite among God's people. This is basic Christianity. It is a standard of Christlikeness of temperament that is available to all God's people. May the Holy Spirit powerfully set about the task of producing in us, whatever our natural temperament, the fruit of the Spirit which is a long temper.

The Law of Kindness

"The fruit of the Spirit is . . . gentleness."
Galatians 5:22

Our Authorized Version uses the word *gentleness* to translate the Greek *chrestotes*, which simply means "kindness." It carries the idea of our being sweet or benign in our attitudes and actions toward others. John Calvin translated it "civility" or "courtesy" and said that by it "we render ourselves amiable." Calvin went on to say that this grace therefore "is chiefly in countenance and word." That is, it is demonstrated in how we approach and treat other people. Archbishop Trench in his work on the synonyms of the New Testament strongly disagrees with this statement. He insists that gentleness or kindness denotes a grace "pervading and penetrating the whole nature, mellowing there all that is harsh or austere." It is always a little perplexing when two eminent linguists disagree. However, we do not have to choose between Calvin and Trench. Each view has a vital element of truth in it. Calvin does not deny that this is an internal grace. What he says is that the usage of the word shows that it chiefly manifests itself in our attitudes, words, and actions toward others. In this he is undoubtedly correct. However, we should never forget Trench's comment that this grace starts deep within us with the sanctifying work of the Holy Spirit.

Perhaps the clearest commentary on the statement "the fruit of the Spirit is gentleness [kindness]" is in the Bible verse with which we ended the last chapter, Ephesians 4:32: "Be ye kind [Greek, *chrestoi*] one to another, tenderhearted, forgiving one another, even as God for Christ's sake hath forgiven you." We see an illustration of this command, in both a positive and a negative way, in the parable of the unmerciful servant in Matthew 18:23–35. The Lord Jesus described a servant who owed his master an enormous sum of money. Facing imprisonment and torture—and in those days the torturers used every exquisite means to put all possible pressure on the debtor and his family to force them to pay up everything they could—the servant cried, "Lord, have patience with me, and I will pay thee all." Of course, he never could have paid it, but his master had pity on him "and loosed him, and forgave him the debt" (verse 27). Out of the sheer kindness of his master the servant received forgiveness.

Now we see the opposite. That same servant went out and met another servant who owed him a paltry little pittance, about one-six-hundred-thousandth of what he had been forgiven. He grabbed his inferior servant by the throat and said, "Pay me that thou owest" (verse 28). The servant said to him what he had said to the master, "Have patience with me, and I will pay thee all" (verse 29). But he would not do it. Instead, he took him and threw him to the torturers to exact his pound of flesh. What this servant did is the opposite of the kindness Paul speaks of in our text. The message of the Lord Jesus in Matthew 18, indeed the message of all the Scriptures, is that we are like the servant with the enormous debt. We owed God such a debt that we were entirely without any means of paying it. Yet out of His own kindness of heart He forgave us the debt in its totality. It behooves us, therefore, to treat other people as the Lord has treated us. The Lord Jesus goes on to say that if we do not forgive men, it is evident that God has not forgiven us. It is not that God forgives us because of our merit in forgiving others, but that all whom He forgives receive His Spirit and the fruit of the Spirit is kindness. If this fruit of the Spirit is absent it can only be because the Spirit is absent. That is a solemn thought for, as Paul says, "If any man have not the Spirit of Christ, he is none of his" (Romans 8:9).

So the simple meaning of the text is that if the Holy Spirit lives and operates in our hearts He will sweeten our disposition so that we will be kind to others for Christ's sake, treating them as God our Father has treated us. This goes right to the heart of practical biblical Christianity. It discovers the reality of our profession of faith in Christ, because if we are really saved the indwelling Holy Spirit will do two things. First, He will sweeten even the most bitter disposition. Second, having done so, He will establish in us what the book of Proverbs terms "the law of kindness" (Proverbs 31:26).

Liberty from Bitterness

The Holy Spirit gives us liberty from bitterness. Bitterness, sourness, and harshness are marks of the flesh that stand in stark contrast with the sweet fruit of kindness. They are not acceptable characteristics in any Christian. They are great sins that do much damage to the Lord's work and to the Lord's people.

The Curse of Bitterness

Bitterness is the peculiar mark of the unconverted "whose mouth is full of cursing and bitterness" (Romans 3:14). It should never characterize the converted. James bluntly asserts, "If ye have bitter envying and strife in your hearts, glory not, and lie not against the truth. This wisdom descendeth not from above, but is earthly, sensual, devilish" (James 3:14–15). Christians often delude themselves that their bitter, sour, harsh, unkind, or ungenerous words and actions are motivated by a superior spirituality. But they arise from another source. There is nothing heavenly about them. The wisdom that produces them and the logic that defends them are earthly, sensual, and devilish. That is, a bitter spirit gives expression to the desires of the world, of the flesh, and of the devil. So bitterness should not characterize a Christian. To the extent that it does, it will exact a high price.

Bitterness blights our homes and churches and is especially evident where there is an unforgiving spirit. Paul warned us to keep bitterness out of our homes: "Husbands love your wives, and be not bitter against them" (Colossians 3:19). When we allow our sour moods to cast a shadow over the home we rob our family of the liberty and joy that they have a right to expect there. We make home a place to be dreaded and drive our loved ones away from us and possibly away from the Saviour.

Concerning the church Paul commands, "Let all bitterness, and wrath, and anger, and clamour, and evil speaking, be put away from you, with all malice: and be ye kind one to another, tenderhearted, forgiving one another, even as God for Christ's sake hath forgiven you" (Ephesians 4:31–32). Wrath, anger, clamor, evil speaking, and malice are the inevitable accompaniments of bitterness, whether in the home or in the church. In many churches they have been the means of hindering a good work for God and have made the house of God more like a synagogue of Satan.

Bitterness brings trouble and defilement to everything and everyone it touches. Solomon says, "There is that speaketh like the piercings of a sword" (Proverbs 12:18). We have all met the kind of person Solomon had in mind. Every word he speaks is razor sharp. It lacerates, it wounds, it hurts. If there are ninety-nine good things to say about someone and one little paltry thing that this person thinks does not measure up, he will ignore all that is laudable and spend his time sticking the piercing sword into the one little flaw. If we turn our tongues into a piercing sword, is it any wonder that we spread defilement and injury among our brethren? We are warned in Hebrews 12:15 to look "diligently lest any man fail of the grace of God; lest any root of bitterness springing up trouble you, and thereby many be defiled." In James 3:16 we are told, "Where envying and strife is, there is confusion and every evil work." Bitterness causes unspeakable damage to all it touches.

Worst of all, bitterness is a blatant denial of all that we profess in Christ. Like the unmerciful servant in our Lord's parable, we profess to have received great forgiveness. We profess even more, for we profess to be like Christ and to bear His name before the world. Yet what could more unlike the Saviour than a bitter spirit, even if we mingle many good and spiritual exercises with it? James described this anomaly: "Out of the same mouth proceedeth blessing and cursing. My brethren, these things ought not so to be. Doth a fountain send forth at the same place sweet water and bitter?" (James 3:10–11).

The Causes of Bitterness

It is the work of the Holy Spirit to give us liberty from the bondage of bitterness. Bitterness belongs to the flesh. The Holy Spirit replaces bitterness with spiritual sweetness. He does so by releasing us from the things that cause people to be bitter. The Bible reveals many causes of bitterness.

Sometimes it is a feeling of one's own superiority that makes a man bitter and sour. Filled with pride, he harshly despises and dismisses others as beneath his dignity. The Pharisees were prime examples of such bitterness. Their treatment of publicans and sinners—and even of the weak and suffering—was the direct result of their "holier-than-thou" attitude. The Pharisee in Christ's parable said to God, "God, I thank thee, that I am not as other men are, extortioners, unjust, adulterers, or even as this publican" (Luke 18:11). Such self-righteous arrogance has no place in a Christian for the first thing the gospel does is to lower the pride of man into the dust before God. It creates in him the opposite spirit from the Pharisee's, so that he cries, "O God, I am a sinner and if there is one person in all of this world who deserves to be punished in hell, I am that person." Those who treat others as inferior are often most proud of the things that they had least part in obtaining, such as intelligence, nationality, color, beauty, health, or even grace. In all these things we are the recipients of God's kindness. Why then should we deal in harsh pride with those who do not enjoy what we have received?

Wounded pride is an especially fertile ground for producing a bitter spirit. Solomon tells us, "A brother offended is harder to be won than a strong city: and their contentions are like the bars of a castle" (Proverbs 18:19). When our pride is offended we tend to strike out in anger or to become sullen and withdrawn. Some people allow this spirit to fester until it becomes habitual and casts its grim shadow over all their dealings with others. While there is sound wisdom in such maxims as "Once bitten, twice shy," it is foolish for us to allow the insults or injuries inflicted by one person to make us sour and suspicious in our dealings with everyone. Yet that is precisely what many do. They allow wounded pride to condemn them to the dark prison of an embittered existence.

Another cause of bitterness is envy. King Saul is a good example of this. He was full of bitterness against David because he envied him. He saw in David the kind of man he wanted to be and wasn't. He was jealous of the praise that David earned of the people. He was envious of David's gifts and feared that David would take over the leadership of Israel. This envy ate away at him until it drove him mad and led him to attempted murder. Because of envy, Saul condemned himself to ceaseless misery. He condemned his family to endless division and discord. He condemned David to years of wandering from his native land and that at a time when his land most needed his military leadership. And Saul condemned his people to years of civil disturbance, leading to wholesale suffering and slaughter. Well did Solomon say, "Jealousy is cruel as the grave: the coals thereof are coals of fire, which hath a most vehement flame" (Song of Solomon 8:6).

Resentment is another cause of bitterness. This was the reason for the bitterness that consumed the prophet Jonah. Jonah spoke bitterly even to God. He was angry with God because he resented God's kindness to the Assyrians, whom he hated as a threat to Israel's security. It was this angry resentment that made Jonah so bitter. In Galatians 5 we notice that the grace of gentleness or kindness follows immediately in the train of longsuffering or "long temper." Short temper leads to bitterness.

Sometimes bitterness arises out of frustration or disappointment. Moses discovered this to be true. The Israelites "provoked his spirit, so that he spake unadvisedly with his lips" (Psalm 106:33). Moses had to pay dearly for his frustration and consequent bitterness for he was denied entry into the promised land. Jeremiah was another man of God whose frustration led him to bitterness, at least for a time. Disappointed and frustrated at the response to his ministry he spoke bitterly to God: "Wilt thou be altogether unto me as a liar?" (Jeremiah 15:18). It is difficult to imagine a prophet speaking to God in this fashion, but when a great man becomes frustrated and disappointed even he is likely to give vent.

Unfulfilled hopes and dreams often give rise to bitterness. "The desire accomplished is sweet to the soul" (Proverbs 13:19), but unaccomplished it is often a bitterness in the bones. The man who feels himself a failure will all too often become sour and critical of those who succeed where he did not.

Fear may produce a bitter spirit, as may extreme suffering. Job is a good example. He was not naturally a bitter man but, worn down by suffering and by the fatigue of an overburdened life, he became bitter against God and men.

In many of these cases we can understand and may be tempted to excuse the sin of bitterness. We would be wrong to do so, because *ultimately bitterness is caused by a breach in our fellowship with God.* Jeremiah says, "It is an evil thing and bitter that thou has forsaken the Lord thy God" (Jeremiah 2:19). As long as we are enjoying the intimacy of fellowship with God, even if we are disappointed in those around us or are suffering in body and mind, we will not become bitter. We will have "songs in the night" (Job 35:10), our meditation of the Lord will be sweet (Psalm 104:34), His words will be sweet to our taste (Psalm 119:103), and we shall account His will to be "good, and acceptable, and perfect" (Romans 12:2).

On the other hand, when we are not living in fellowship with God, we are likely to fall into bitterness. This is because bitterness is often the result of unresolved guilt. We may gather this from Jeremiah's words: "Thy way and thy doings have procured these things unto thee; this is thy wickedness, because it is bitter, because it reacheth unto thine heart" (Jeremiah 4:18). Sin produces bitter consequences, but it also causes us to become bitter in our treatment of others. Haunted by a sense of our own guilt, we are apt to find fault with others and to seek to take out our guilt on them.

These are some of the things that cause bitterness. In every case, they tend to make us careless about the face we present to other people and about how we speak to them. Our own inward feelings produce attitudes, words, and actions that are harsh, unkind, or thoughtless.

The Cure for Bitterness

The Holy Spirit's answer to bitterness in a Christian is twofold. *First, the Holy Spirit lays the foundation for changing our sour disposition by leading us into a true enjoyment of Christ and of the pardon we have in Him.* We have been emphasizing the words of Ephesians 4:32, where Paul joins our freedom from bitterness with God's kindness to us: "Be ye kind one to another, tenderhearted, forgiving one another, even as God for Christ's sake hath forgiven you." If only we would live in the enjoyment of God's total, absolute, perfect, and everlasting pardon through the merits of Christ's blood, we would experience victory over pride, envy, resentment, frustration, fear, and guilt. Such an experience would be even more potent than physical sufferings. Some of the most joyful people I have known have been people who have lived with a high level of perpetual bodily suffering. They have been consumed, not with bitterness because of pain, but with blessedness because of pardon. David rejoiced, "Blessed is he whose transgression is forgiven, whose sin is covered. Blessed is the man unto whom the Lord imputeth not iniquity, and in whose spirit there is no guile" (Psalm 32:1–2). This inward joy is the certain cure for sourness. A fresh and compelling view of God's pardon "for Christ's sake" is the key to escaping bitterness.

Second, having laid the foundation by leading us to enjoy our pardon in Christ, the Holy Spirit causes an actual change in us. That is, He accomplishes in us the work of sanctification by which He makes a real change in us. He gives us the desire to have unimpeded fellowship with God. Though *we* may not feel grieved by the harsh things we say and do to other people or by our surly disposition, God is and He lets us know it. We feel the loss of fellowship and long for it to be restored and for every hindrance to it to be removed.

Not only does the Spirit gives us a desire for unimpeded fellowship with God, He also gives us a desire to be good representatives of the Lord Jesus Christ. He makes us see that the best thing we can do in the world is to set Christ before men. When the Holy Spirit sets this conviction in our hearts, He has us on the way to real holiness, including real gentleness, or kindness. A harsh and bitter person cannot be a good representative of Christ. Whatever talents a bitter person possesses, what can anyone ever see of Christ in him? If we desire to be Christ's representatives we must bear this fruit of kindness.

The Holy Spirit goes beyond giving us a desire to be good representatives of Christ and actually convicts us of our sin and changes us into the image of our Saviour. We have already referred to Paul's words in 2 Corinthians 3:18 but they will bear repeating: "We all, with open face beholding as in a glass the glory of the Lord, are changed into the same image from glory to glory, even as by the Spirit of the Lord." This is not an overnight work or a sudden achievement of sinless perfection. Sanctification is an ongoing work. Moses, Jeremiah, Job, and Jonah were not habitually bitter men, but neither were they sinless. Each of them sinned by becoming bitter. Similarly, Christians are not sinless but neither are they habitually bitter. When Paul wrote, "Be ye kind one to another," he meant, "Become kind one to another." He recognized that Christlike kindness is not brought to perfection all at once. We are real people with real faults and real feelings, but the Holy Spirit can and will give us liberty from bitterness.

The Law of Kindness

When He gives us liberty from bitterness, the Spirit establishes in us the law of kindness. That is one of the most beautiful expressions of Scripture. In Proverbs 31:26 it is given as a description of the virtuous woman, and among her many charms I don't think there is one greater than this, "She openeth her mouth with wisdom; and in her tongue is the law of kindness." That law is precisely what Paul has laid down in Ephesians 4:32: We must treat others for Christ's sake as God has treated us for His sake. The Lord has been kind to us, has He not? Where would we be today if God had not been kind to us? If He had been harsh or austere toward us, or if He had been strict to mark iniquity, where would we be today? We would all be lost in the outer darkness of hell. But He has been kind to us. He has dealt with us with His eye on Christ. That is how the Lord deals with His people. He never forgets that we are in Christ. He never deals with us apart from Christ and therefore He gives us a full, free, and unconditional pardon. He admits us into His fellowship, speaking to us words of grace, kindness, and encouragement.

The law of kindness tells us how we are to treat others. For Christians, this is a divine law. It is the rule, not the exception. If we are sour the trouble is in us, not in those around us. The trouble is not in our circumstances but in our hearts. Our sourness hurts others and defames the Lord Jesus Christ. It evidences our lack of joy in and likeness to Christ. Bitterness can be replaced with kindness only as the Holy Spirit applies the gospel to our souls. Kindness is the fruit of the Spirit. That means that the Holy Spirit can actually effect such a change in us as to produce the image of Christ in us. He can make the law of kindness the rule of our lives as we live in the joy of how God has treated us for Christ's sake.

Tough Love

"The fruit of the Spirit is . . . goodness."
Galatians 5:22

The word *goodness* sounds deceptively simple. Actually, in Galatians 5:22 the Greek word *agathosune* that is translated "goodness" is notoriously difficult to define. The problem is that we have very little data to go on. The word does not appear in secular Greek literature and it occurs only four times in the New Testament, though the adjective *agathos* occurs more than one hundred times. Ordinarily, its meaning is plain. It may mean kindness, but that is not its meaning in our text because the word that immediately precedes it means kindness. *Goodness* may speak of the cardinal virtue of uprightness of character; that is, it may describe internal holiness or Godlikeness. The English words *good* and *God* are from the same root so that goodness as a description of character properly signifies Godlikeness. However, while it would be quite true to say that the fruit of the Spirit is holiness or uprightness, that obviously cannot be the meaning in Galatians 5:22, because uprightness of character and holiness are nothing less than the combination of all the nine virtues that constitute the fruit of the Spirit. All of them add up to true holiness or uprightness of character; goodness is just one aspect of that holiness.

So what does *goodness* signify? Even expert linguists have a difficult time distinguishing between it and the term that immediately precedes it. It is very closely related in meaning to the Greek word *chrestotes*, which is translated "gentleness" or "kindness." In fact, secular Greek grammarians were wont to deny to *agathosune* ("goodness"), all right to exist. They saw neither need nor place for it in the language because, as they believed, it said nothing that *chrestotes* did not say and it was a much inferior word. These grammarians were wrong. There *is* a difference between the words in question and it must be well worth noting for the Holy Spirit to place them side by side in Galatians 5:22.

Jerome, who translated the Bible from Hebrew and Greek into what became the Latin Vulgate version, sought to show the different shades of meaning in the words. A simplified paraphrase of his view is that kindness is the virtue that acts spontaneously to do good to others. Goodness also sets out to do good to others, but with this difference: it always pursues what is of real benefit to its object; it is truly kind, even when it appears to be severe. There are times when we must be cruel to be kind. In the light of this distinction, it is significant that Paul adds goodness to kindness. He is speaking of a particular type of kindness— *godly kindness.*

That is the ultimate force of the word *goodness* in our text. It is not mere softness. It is not doing what others wish or expect us to do. Goodness is doing what is really for their good, what has become popularly known "tough love." It is the virtue of always being available to be of true service and true usefulness to others.

We gain added insight into the full significance of goodness from Paul's words in 2 Thessalonians 1:11: "Wherefore also we pray always for you, that our God would count you worthy of this calling, and fulfil all the good pleasure of his goodness, and the work of faith with power." The phrase "the good pleasure of His goodness" has the plain meaning of "the agreeable, beneficial, or useful purpose of God's kindness" towards us. This leads us to the conclusion that goodness describes not merely an action of doing good to others, but also the deep inner motive from which our actions of kindness must spring.

To summarize, by the word *goodness* in Galatians 5:22 Paul means the aim and action of a Christian to be of real service to other people and to do them good. "The fruit of the Spirit is . . . goodness." That is, the Holy Spirit works in a Christian to make him a true instrument of good in the world. We will emphasize three actions of the Spirit by which He accomplishes this.

The Holy Spirit Teaches Us What Is Truly Good
First, the Holy Spirit teaches us what is truly good. What is good and beneficial must be defined by the word of God and not by the

opinions of men. This is very important. What is good can never be ungodly or contrary to the word of God. Goodness is the fruit of the Spirit and the Spirit does not lead men contrary to His own word. The Scripture's command is "Hear what the Spirit saith unto the churches," and the only way we can do that is by attending to His written and authoritative word, the Bible.

Nowadays it is popular to berate Christians for their alleged lack of love and kindness. For example, our refusal to accept sodomites and to condone their lifestyle is attacked as judgmental and unkind. Similarly, any stand we take against false religion is labeled bigoted and harsh (the criticism becomes hysterical if we dare to evaluate the Church of Rome by the teachings of Scripture). We have reached the stage where even attempts to evangelize are condemned as an expression of hatred. Many in the media joined in condemning Southern Baptists because they prayed for Jews to be converted to Christ and distributed literature to introduce them to the gospel of Christ. It meant nothing to the critics that there are no people less antagonistic to the Jewish people and to Israel than the evangelical community, including the Southern Baptists. The Baptists were unkind because they dared to pray for the conversion of Jews. In the view of many anthropologists, the kindest thing that the church can do for the world's primitive tribes is to stop sending missionaries and to leave the cultural heritage of the heathen undisturbed.

More than ever we need to have a divine definition of what is truly good. Samuel, as God's prophet and spokesman, said to the Israelites, "I will teach you the good and the right way" (1 Samuel 12:23). What is that good way? In the days of Moses, Israel grasped the answer to that question, at least for a time: "The thing which thou hast spoken is good for us to do" (Deuteronomy 1:14). Let me tell you, that is always true; that is the rule for every Christian: What God has spoken is good for us to do. As Moses confirmed for Israel, "The Lord commanded us to do all these statutes, to fear the Lord our God, for our good always, that he might preserve us alive, as it is at this day" (Deuteronomy 6:24).

The Holy Spirit defines good in the word of God. In a beautiful statement in the Old Testament as Nehemiah prays to the Lord, he says, "Thou camest down also upon mount Sinai, and spakest with them from heaven, and gavest them right judgments, and true laws, good statutes and commandments . . . . Thou gavest also thy good spirit to instruct them, and withheldest not thy manna from their mouth, and gavest them water for their thirst" (Nehemiah 9:13, 20).

If our kindness toward people is to ascend to the level of goodness, it must be governed by the word of God. Kindness therefore demands that we oppose all that is against God or His word because what is antagonistic to God is harmful to men. Only when we live and act by the standards of the word of God does our kindness become goodness.

The Holy Spirit Teaches Us Goodness from the Greatest Example of It

The second action of the Holy Spirit in making us instruments of good in the world is to teach us from the greatest possible example of true goodness, namely the Lord Jesus Christ. Peter, an eyewitness, described the ministry of the Lord Jesus: "God anointed Jesus of Nazareth with the Holy Spirit and power: who went about doing good" (Acts 10:38). This is how the Holy Spirit summarizes the ministry of the Saviour: He went about doing good. Lives, homes, and entire communities were changed for the better by the Lord Jesus Christ's going among them and doing good. The Lord Jesus Himself said, "The Son of Man came not to be ministered unto [or, to be served], but to minister, and to give his life a ransom for many" (Matthew 20:28).

The life of Christ was a life of self-abnegation: "He made Himself of no reputation" (Philippians 2:7). It was a life of sacrifice and of self-surrender. His purpose was always to do good to men for time and for eternity. The Gospels are full of illustrations of this goodness. When He went to the pool of Bethesda and gave the impotent man the power to rise up and walk, He was doing good. When He gave sight to the blind or hearing to the deaf, when He raised the dead to life, He was doing good. We can all recognize His goodness in these miraculous acts. Those who benefited from them had no doubt that the Lord Jesus had done them good. But He just as truly "went about doing good" when He drove the sellers out of the temple as when He was doing those miracles. He was still going about doing good when He withstood the Pharisees, calling them "Scribes, Pharisees, hypocrites," as when he broke the bread and fish to feed the multitude. The Lord Jesus is our example of a life of self-sacrifice set for the good of others. What motivated Him is what motivates all true goodness. We are not left to speculate about the hidden spring from which all His actions flowed: "The zeal of thine house hath eaten me up" (John 2:17).

A zeal for the glory of God as it is revealed in the word of God and exemplified by the Son of God is the strongest and surest compulsion a Christian can know to "do good unto all men" (Galatians 6:10). It will assure two things. First, that we will do good. It will not allow us to sit at ease, doing nothing for the good of our fellow men, indifferent to their plight and careless about their needs. Second, it will insure that we never substitute a social program for the full-orbed service of the gospel. It will govern the activities we undertake and keep us from falling away from true Christian goodness to the empty sentimentality of humanism that is content to help with people's temporal needs without addressing their spiritual needs. We must aim at reflecting the goodness of Christ. Nothing less is worthy of the description "the fruit of the Spirit."

The Holy Spirit Gives Us a True Servant Spirit

The third thing the Holy Spirit does to produce the fruit of goodness in us is to impart to us a true servant spirit. It is impossible to be a Christian without becoming like Christ, and it is impossible to become like Christ without becoming a servant, for He is preeminently the Servant of the Lord. Servanthood is the very essence of sainthood. There is no higher calling or privilege than to serve. Paul happily identified himself as "a servant of Jesus Christ, called to be an apostle" (Romans 1:1). Apostleship was not exemption from servanthood, but an intensification of it. Being a servant calls for a life of self-denial, self-sacrifice, and self-surrender in order to do good to others in the name of our Saviour. In our society that kind of life is despised. The philosophy that governs the attitudes and actions of many is the primacy of self-interest. Virtues such as selflessness, humility, and altruistic kindness are dismissed as weakness. Christians must stand opposed to this denial of the ethics and example of our Saviour. We will discover that what was true of Christ continues to be true of all who follow Him: The price of doing sinners good is to become a servant. Any man who wants his life to count for God must humble himself to be a genuine servant. Does not our Lord tell us that at His return He will say, "Well done, good and faithful *servant*" (Matthew 25:23) to those who have done the will of God? Narrow self-interest pays no dividend that will stand the test of eternity. Only genuine service that arises out of faith in and love for Christ produces that "treasure in heaven" of which Jesus spoke in the Sermon on the Mount (Matthew 6:19).

Thus, in producing goodness in us the Holy Spirit gives us a servant spirit. In doing so—and always according to the station in which God sovereignly places us to serve Him—He impresses on us something of the revelation of Christ to the newly-converted Saul of Tarsus: "I have appeared unto thee for this purpose, to make thee a minister and a witness both of these things which thou hast seen, and of those things in the which I will appear unto thee; delivering thee from the people, and from the Gentiles, unto whom now I send thee, to open their eyes, and to turn them from darkness to light, and from the power of Satan unto God, that they may receive forgiveness of sins, and inheritance among them which are sanctified by faith that is in me" (Acts 26:16–18). While it is not the work of the Spirit to make every Christian an apostle Paul, it is His work to stir up every Christian to embrace this challenge in some degree. Christ revealed Himself to Paul to make him a minister, a servant—the Greek word *huperetes* (literally, "an under-rower" as distinct from *nautes*, "a seaman") signifies an attendant, a subordinate servant who acts under the orders of another. This is the calling of every Christian. By producing the fruit of goodness in us the Holy Spirit brings us to the place of giving up our carnal self-assertiveness to place ourselves under the direct command of our Master. In stirring us to embrace this servant calling, the Holy Spirit will accomplish three things in us.

Spreading the Gospel

He will give us the desire to spread the gospel. In calling us to be servants He calls us to be witnesses to lead men to Christ. Can we do any greater good to men than to invade their darkness with the light of the glorious gospel of Christ? Paul felt the urgency of such a good work. "If our gospel be hid, it is hid to them that are lost: in whom the god of this world hath blinded the minds of them which believe not, lest the light of the glorious gospel of Christ, who is the image of God, should shine unto them" (2 Corinthians 4:3–4). This is the urgency that burns in every good man's heart. He feels something of the apostle's burden: "Necessity is laid upon me; yea, woe is unto me, if I preach not the gospel!" (1 Corinthians 9:16). Goodness has a vital interest in spreading the gospel. It is essentially a missionary virtue. It cannot sit still while all around people are perishing with no man to care for their souls.

Bringing Others to Heaven

Goodness is not only a missionary virtue, it is a virtue that concentrates on eternity more than on time. Thus when the Holy Spirit produces the fruit of goodness in us He gives us a heart to bring others to heaven. There is an old hymn that captures something of this spirit:

> We're going home to glory soon,
> To see the city bright;
> To walk the golden streets of heav'n
> And bask in God's own light.
> But some of you are out of Christ
> And held by many a snare;
> We cannot leave you lost and lone,
> We want you over there.

As he led Israel toward the promised land Moses expressed this very sentiment to his father-in-law: "We are journeying unto the place of which the Lord said, I will give it you: come thou with us, and we will do thee good: for the Lord hath spoken good concerning Israel" (Numbers 10:29). This is precisely the testimony of every believer in the Lord Jesus Christ. We are traveling to the land that our Saviour has promised to us (John 14:1–3). It is natural for us to desire to bring as many with us as we can. Paul had this burden: "I am made all things to all men, that I might by all means save some" (1 Corinthians 9:22). Good men do not squander all their time and effort on things that will perish after a few years. Rather, they serve for eternity. They know that they will leave every gain of earth behind them. The only things from this world that can accompany us to heaven are the souls we have won for Christ. Goodness seeks to "save some." It is a heaven-oriented virtue.

Interest in the Household of Faith

Goodness is also a family virtue. In producing this godly kindness in us the Holy Spirit leads us to spend ourselves in the interests of the household of faith. The Scripture commands: "As we have therefore opportunity, let us do good unto all men, especially unto them who are of the household of faith" (Galatians 6:10). Good men will seek to do good on all fronts, but their special interest is in the church of Christ. Christians bearing the fruit of the Spirit will be to the household of faith what the virtuous woman of Proverbs 31 is to her natural household: "Who can find a virtuous woman? for her price is far above rubies. The heart of her husband doth safely trust in her, so that he shall have no need of spoil. She will do him good and not evil all the days of her life" (Proverbs 31:10–12). Then follows a catalogue of activity, industry, and selfless service. What a life of activity! This description of a woman's work is possibly what gave rise to the saying, "A woman's work is never done." Why does a good wife do all this work? The answer is simple: to a good woman, to do good to her husband and to her house is the greatest fulfillment of God's purpose for her existence. The same is true of all of us in the household of faith. What it true goodness? It is every Christian doing for the household of faith what a virtuous woman does for her house.

"The fruit of the Spirit is . . . goodness." This goodness—this godly kindness—is a holy zeal to do men good by leading them to Christ and by serving and edifying them once they are in the body of Christ. It is a zeal that is pure and selfless. It is courageous enough to do what is right and truly beneficial rather than what is easy or popular. It is the virtue that most clearly imitates the Lord Jesus Christ in the great work of furthering the kingdom of God among men.

"He hath shewed thee, O man, what is good; and what doth the Lord require of thee, but to do justly, and to love mercy, and to walk humbly with thy God?" (Micah 6:8).

Trust and Trustworthiness

"The fruit of the Spirit is . . . faith."
Galatians 5:22

Commentators are almost unanimous that the word *faith* in this text does not mean trust in God or in the gospel. Admitting that that is the usual meaning of the word, they point out that there are other places where it obviously carries the idea of trustworthiness, faithfulness, or honesty. For example, when Paul posed the question, "What if some did not believe? shall their unbelief make the faith of God without effect?" (Romans 3:3), he meant, "Does the fact that Israel refused to believe God's promise nullify His faithfulness?" Again, describing the kind of behavior expected of Christian servants, Paul wrote, "Exhort servants to be obedient unto their own masters, and to please them well in all things; not answering again; not purloining, but shewing all good fidelity [Greek *pistis*, 'faith']; that they may adorn the doctrine of God our Saviour in all things" (Titus 2:9–10). We readily recognize this use of the word, for we equate honesty with "good faith." That is precisely what Paul meant. Christians should be trustworthy; they should show good faith in all their dealings. Most commentators hold that when the apostle included *pistis* as a virtue listed under the fruit of the Spirit he meant faithfulness, integrity, or trustworthiness.

Despite the near unanimity of the commentators, the arguments advanced to sustain their interpretation are not altogether conclusive. One argument is that Paul cannot intend us to understand faith as trust here because in a theological sense faith is the basis of all the virtues in the list. Even to state this contention is to show its weakness. It is a bald assertion, for it is far from self-evident that faith includes all the other listed virtues. If we had to say of faith what we said of holiness in the last chapter, that it is the sum total of all the other virtues, then it would have to be excluded. But this is not borne out by Scripture or experience. Faith is indeed a foundational virtue, but the notion that a foundational virtue has no place in the list is false. This is proved by the fact that love (which all admit to be a foundational virtue) stands at the head of the list. Thus the argument that faith in its theological sense has no place in the list because it is a foundational virtue, is demonstrably false.

A second argument that faith cannot mean trust is taken from where it appears in the list. It occupies, we are told, a lowly position relative to the other virtues. Had Paul been referring to faith in the Lord and His word, surely he would have given the word a much more prominent position. Therefore, it is argued, he was speaking not of faith but of personal integrity or faithfulness. This argument is as inconclusive as the first. The placement of faith in this list of virtues arises from the apostle's structure, not from any supposed inferiority in the term itself. The nine virtues fall into three groups that trace the fruit of the Spirit in developing Christian character in three directions: upward toward God, outward toward man, and inward toward ourselves. The first word of each group is its controlling word. Love controls joy and peace; longsuffering controls kindness and goodness, and faith controls meekness and temperance. So the placement of faith has a good reason and arises from the writer's design.

It is best to give the word the full scope of its meaning. It may be objected that to do this flies in the face of a fundamental law of interpretation, namely, that a text or a term has a single meaning. In other words, the Scripture writers had a definite meaning in mind—or at least the Spirit who inspired them had a definite meaning in mind—when they wrote. It is the interpreter's job to find out from the language they used what the writers' meaning was. It is unjustifiable to stretch their language to make it mean a variety of things. This is a necessary canon and one that we must not cast off. We must never fall into the trap of reducing Scripture interpretation to "what this text means to me." We must insist respectfully that it does not really matter what this text means to me, *what matters is what it really means!* To give *faith* its full range of meaning in Galatians 5:22 does not violate this canon. The Holy Spirit was well aware of the range of the word when He inspired Paul to employ it in a context that did not limit its meaning either to "faith" or "faithfulness." The single sense of the text then is that the Holy Spirit makes His people trusting and trustworthy. This is what Paul means when he says, "The fruit of the Spirit is . . . faith."

A Trusting People

The Holy Spirit makes His people a trusting people. The Bible specifically calls the Holy Spirit "the Spirit of faith." In 2 Corinthians 4:13 we have this statement: "We having the same spirit of faith, according as it is written, I believed, and therefore have I spoken; we also believe, and therefore speak." Commenting on this text Charles Hodge remarked,

> "The spirit of faith" may be a periphrase [a round-about expression] for faith itself; or the word spirit may refer to the human spirit, and the whole mean "having the same believing spirit." It is more in accordance with scriptural usage, and especially with Paul's manner, to make spirit refer to the Holy Spirit, who is so often designated from the effects which he produces. He is called the Spirit of adoption, Rom. 8:15; the Spirit of wisdom, Eph. 1:17; the Spirit of grace, Heb. 10:29; the Spirit of glory, 1 Pet. 4:14. The apostle means to say that [he also possessed] the same blessed Spirit which was the author of faith in David (*Commentary on The Second Epistle to the Corinthians*).

"The Spirit of faith" is an appropriate title for the Holy Spirit for three reasons.

Saving Faith

First, the Holy Spirit enables His people to believe to the saving of their souls. Saving faith is the gift of God and is the direct result of the regenerating act of the Holy Spirit upon their spiritually dead souls. Saving faith is not some inherent power that resides in the free will of man. Man's freedom of will is freedom to sin. He has no ability to orig-inate spiritual good. The Lord Jesus spoke of man's will as refusing to embrace Him: "Ye will not [that is, 'are not willing to'] come to me, that ye might have life" (John 5:40). Saving faith is the result of the Spirit's act of regeneration. Consider these truths:

- *The natural man cannot even discover the gospel.* When Simon Peter confessed, "Thou art the Christ, the Son of the living God," Jesus said, "Blessed art thou, Simon Barjona: for flesh and blood hath not revealed it unto thee, but my Father which is in heaven" (Matthew 16:17). On another occasion our Lord said, "No man knoweth the Son, but the Father; neither knoweth any man the Father, save the Son, and he to whomsoever the Son will [literally, 'may purpose or choose to'] reveal him" (Matthew 11:27). When he chooses to reveal Himself to a person He does so by the effectual working of His Spirit. Only the Spirit can make Christ known savingly to men. This is His ministry: "He shall glorify me: for he shall receive of mine, and shall shew it unto you" (John 16:14).

- *The natural man cannot respond believingly to the gospel.* Jesus said, "No man can come to me, except the Father which hath sent me draw him" (John 6:44). Why can he not come? There can be no doubt that every hearer of the gospel should come to Christ. Everyone should obey the commands of Scripture to repent and believe the gospel and embrace the promise that the Lord will receive everyone who comes to Him (John 6:37). But the fact is that in the depraved soul of every man by nature there is such an antipathy to God, such a deadness to the things of God, such a willful inability to choose spiritual good, that even when the truth is given to him the natural man cannot believe it. As Paul said, "The natural man receiveth not the things of the Spirit of God: for they are foolishness unto him: neither can he know them, because they are spiritually discerned" (1 Corinthians 2:14).

- Thus *the Holy Spirit enlightens the mind and renews the will of each one He brings into salvation in Christ.* We read of "the work of faith with power" (2 Thessalonians 1:11). The power that it takes to produce faith in us is that which raised Christ from the dead. Paul wrote to the Ephesians about "the exceeding greatness of his power to us-ward who believe, according to the working of his mighty power, which he wrought in Christ, when he raised him from the dead, and set him at his own right hand in the heavenly places" (Ephesians 1:19–20). He terms our entrance into salvation a resurrection from the dead: "You hath he quickened, who were dead in trespasses and sins" (Ephesians 2:1). This is the only truly biblical way of understanding what happens in a sinner to bring him to faith in Christ. Ezekiel's prophecy has a personal fulfillment in everyone whom the Lord saves: "A new heart also will I give you, and a new spirit will I put within you: and I will take away the stony heart out of your flesh, and I will give you an heart of flesh" (Ezekiel 36:26). A new heart, a new spirit—these are what the Holy Spirit gives us when He brings us to life in Christ and enables us to believe savingly in Jesus Christ.

Sanctifying Faith

Second, the Holy Spirit enables His people to keep believing to their sanctification. It is to be feared that multitudes around us are comforting themselves with a false hope, vainly assuring themselves that they are on the way to heaven while in reality they are yet in their sins. They point to a profession of faith, a "decision for Christ," because of which they believe they are saved, though they will admit that their decision has never led to any change of life or real love for Christ. If pressed they may admit to being backsliders. They may even admit to being carnal Christians, but they will insist that they are Christians. Some-times they will put it in these terms: "I have received Christ as my Saviour but not yet as my Lord." Many preachers encourage this sort of delusion, for delusion it is. It is true that even genuinely saved persons sin. Every one of us falls and fails. But beware of the fallacy that relegates faith to an event in the past, the decision of a bygone moment. In the New Testament saving faith is almost always spoken of in the present tense. Notice the careful wording of John 1:12: "As many as received [Greek, aorist tense] him, to them gave he power to become the sons of God, even to them that believe [Greek, 'are believing'] on his name." Receiving Christ is a once-for-all experience that produces a faith that keeps on believing and trusting. A faith that does nothing more than look back to a point in history is not saving faith. Genuine faith enables those who trust in Christ for salvation to keep trusting Him for sanctification. Paul says, "We walk by faith, not by sight" (2 Corinthians 5:7). Observe the famous words of Galatians 2:20: "I am [have been] crucified with Christ: nevertheless I live; yet not I, but Christ liveth in me: and the life which I now live in the flesh I live by the faith of the Son of God, who loved me, and gave himself for me." Notice this carefully: "The life that I now live in the flesh"—isn't that where we all face the problem of the old man—in the flesh? "I live by the faith of [that is, 'by faith in'] the Son of God." By faith in the Christ who died for us we achieve victory over sin. The Spirit who begot faith in us for justification (Romans 5:1) keeps us believing for sanctification. Together these elements constitute genuine faith. One cannot exist without the other. Any person who thinks he has justifying faith when he has never experienced any of the power of sanctifying faith deceives himself.

This truth that sanctification is by a continuing faith in Christ wrought in us by the Holy Spirit is not well understood. Sanctification does not come by the law, or by personal discipline, or even by reading and memorizing the Bible. It comes by faith, which is the fruit of the Spirit. Let there be no misunderstanding. Sanctifying faith will produce obedience to God's law. It will produce self-discipline. It will produce a desire to feast on the word of God, the memorization of which is an undiluted blessing and a powerful impetus to holiness. But none of these things, apart from faith in Christ, will produce any spiritual good. The work of the Spirit is to take the glorious truths of the gospel revealed in Scripture and work them into our hearts so that they become much more than matters of information. Accepted by faith, they provide the motivation we need to do right and to overcome in our battle with the flesh.

All this must be emphasized in opposition to certain mechanical views of the Christian life that have gained widespread acceptance among Bible believers. Many have fallen into a legalistic approach to Christian living. Some openly state, "Justification is by faith; sanctification is by law." Others unwittingly have become just as legalistic, having been influenced by those that proclaim that Christians have nothing to do with the law in any sense. At the same time these very people reduce the Christian life to a series of "principles," which is just another way of saying that it is to be lived by a set of rules or laws. They have rules for everything and many of the rules are man-made—indeed, at times they are merely psychological insights drawn from the works of ungodly psychologists with Bible texts (divorced from their contexts) appended. The theory goes that by following these rules, we practice true holiness. One must admire the sincerity of anyone who makes a serious effort to be holy in this evil world. The trouble with this mechanical approach to sanctification is first, that it leads to bondage and frustration, and second, that it is attempting the impossible: It attempts to create holiness apart from a faith that has immediate recourse to the work of Christ for us.

Sanctification proceeds as the Holy Spirit continues to show us Christ and to apply to our hearts the truth of His gospel and the merits of His work. When we live our lives as a reaction to Calvary—that is, when we face every situation with the question, What does the gospel of Christ dictate that I do in this situation?—we are living by faith. We need not, as too many preachers do, make a great mystery of it. To live by faith is to allow what we believe about the Lord Jesus Christ and His work for us according to the Scriptures to govern how we act. Gospel belief produces Christian behavior because faith is the fruit of the Spirit. Paul wrote of the divine activity that produces true holiness: "Wherefore also we pray always for you, that our God would . . . fulfill [Greek, *pleroo*, 'fill up'] the good pleasure of His goodness, and [that he would also fill up] the work of faith with power" (2 Thessalonians 1:11). The message here is clear. It is the will of God to mature and complete the work of faith in His people.

Specifically, it is the Holy Spirit who accomplishes this work of maturing faith in us. Paul made this clear in writing to the Galatians: "Are ye so foolish? having begun in the Spirit, are ye now made perfect [or, 'brought to maturity'] by the flesh?" (Galatians 3:3). Sanctification is the special work of the Holy Spirit (1 Peter 1:2). It is the Holy Spirit who shows us what God has freely given us in Christ (1 Corinthians 2:10, 12). He empowers us to mortify the flesh (Romans 8:11). He it is who leads us (Romans 8:14; Galatians 5:18) and who witnesses to us of our position in Christ (Romans 8:16).

We are commanded, "Walk in the Spirit, and ye shall not fulfil the lust of the flesh" (Galatians 5:16). That walk is a walk of faith. It is by producing the fruit of faith in us that the Holy Spirit enables us to receive all the benefit of His sanctifying work.

Special Faith

Third, the Holy Spirit imparts special gifts of faith to His people to enable them to embrace the promises of God for particular needs and situations. Among the special gifts of the Spirit, distributed according to God's sovereign will to the members of Christ's body to enable them to fulfill their particular functions, is faith (1 Corinthians 12:9). To stand, as Paul did, on the deck of a sinking ship, with no discernible hope in sight, and say, "Sirs, be of good cheer: for I believe God [that no one would perish]" (Acts 27:25) is the gift of the Spirit of faith. Sooner or later we all must stand on our own version of that sinking ship, when we face extreme difficulties to which there is no apparent solution. In such times we need to know the mind of the Lord and stand on His promise. The Holy Spirit can make His word so real to us that it will come with the force that Paul felt when the Lord stood by him during that storm. When He does, He will give us the grace to stand on His word by naked faith. The gift of special faith to meet special circumstances is not something that God has withdrawn from His church. When we read of the exploits of the heroes of faith in Hebrews 11 we must admit that some of them saw miracles that are not available to us today. For example, we do not see deep seas miraculously dried up, or the defenses of great cities fall down before us, or our dead loved ones raised to life. But not all the special gifts of faith mentioned in that chapter deal with miraculous things. Paul speaks first of those who did the impossible through faith: "What shall I more say? for the time would fail me to tell of Gedeon, and of Barak, and of Samson, and of Jephthae; of David also, and Samuel, and of the prophets: who through faith subdued kingdoms, wrought righteousness, obtained promises, stopped the mouths of lions, quenched the violence of fire, escaped the edge of the sword, out of weakness were made strong, waxed valiant in fight, turned to flight the armies of the aliens" (Hebrews 11:32–34). But then Paul goes on to describe a different class of people. They also exercised the special gift of faith. They were not a whit behind the first class in believing God, but instead of doing the impossible though faith they endured the unendurable through faith: "And others had trial of cruel mockings and scourgings, yea, moreover of bonds and imprisonment: They were stoned, they were sawn asunder, were tempted, were slain with the sword: they wandered about in sheepskins and goatskins; being destitute, afflicted, tormented; (Of whom the world was not worthy:) they wandered in deserts, and in mountains, and in dens and caves of the earth" (Hebrews 11:36–38).

There are times when the Lord gives us faith to believe that He will remove the burden from our shoulders. There are other times when He gives us the faith to believe that He will strengthen our shoulders to bear the burden. His promise to us implies that this will be the norm: "There hath no temptation taken you but such as is common to man: but God is faithful, who will not suffer you to be tempted above that ye are able; but will with the temptation also make a way to escape, that ye may be able to bear it" (1 Corinthians 10:13). Notice that the way of escape is not that we may be able to *avoid* the trial but to *bear* it.

We who are saved by faith cannot live without faith. The Spirit who started us on our way to heaven enables us to "lay aside every weight, and the sin which doth so easily beset us, and . . . run with patience the race that is set before us, looking unto Jesus the author and finisher of our faith" (Hebrews 12:1–2). The Holy Spirit makes His people a trusting people.

A Trustworthy People

The Holy Spirit also makes His people a trustworthy people. He enables them to live out their faith in a life of faithfulness and honesty in all their relationships. Those who are "led of the Spirit" (Galatians 5:18) are people of character. They are not saved because of their character. That would be works salvation, which is a heresy. Rather, they have character because they are saved. Trust in Christ makes us trustworthy because the fruit of the Spirit is faith, which includes both trust and trustworthiness. It is a contradiction in terms to say, "I am trusting Christ, but no one can trust me." When the Holy Spirit gives us faith in Christ He transforms the very root of our being and continues His work in us to transform us into the image of Christ (2 Corinthians 3:18). According to Galatians 5, those who are led by the flesh bring forth the works of the flesh (verses 19–21), while those who are led of the Spirit bring forth the fruit of the Spirit, including trustworthiness or integrity (verses 22–23).

True to God

This means that Christians will characteristically be true to God. They will be like Moses, who "was faithful in all his house" (Hebrews 3:5). Christians do not desert their Lord's standard however hot the battle. If, like Archbishop Cranmer, they find their faith fails them and they compromise their testimony, they will, as he did, bitterly lament their failure and seek forgiveness and restoration. They cannot be like a most inappropriately named officer in the Parliamentary army, Sir Faithful Fortescue, who at the battle of Edgehill deserted his friends and his standard and charged against them with the Royalist commander Prince Rupert. It is the ministry of the Holy Spirit to keep His people true to God.

True to the Gospel

The Holy Spirit also keeps His people true to the gospel. They will be like Tychicus and Epaphras. Tychicus, Paul said, was "a beloved brother and a faithful minister in the Lord" (Ephesians 6:21). Similarly, Epaphras was to the Colossians "a faithful minister of Christ" (Colossians 1:7). This is the fruit of the Spirit in action, producing fidelity to the gospel. We must never deviate from its doctrine, or fail in its proclamation. Archbishop Trench tells the story that a young minister asked the Duke of Wellington, "Does not your grace think it almost useless and absurd to preach the gospel to the Hindus in view of their obstinacy?" The Duke's reply was memorable: "Look, sir, to your marching orders, 'Preach the gospel to every creature.'" This is the calling to which every Christian is called to be faithful.

True to Our Word

A Christian must be true to his own word. Christians are not liars and liars are not Christians. That is evident from the apostle John's stern warning: "All liars shall have their part in the lake which burneth with fire and brimstone" (Revelation 21:8). Christians bear the image of their God and Saviour. He is faithful: "He abideth faithful: he cannot deny himself" (2 Timothy 2:13). Repeatedly His word is declared to be faithful. We may trust what He says and never be put to shame for doing so. So God's people are faithful to their word. This is the fruit of the Spirit in them. David inquired as to the identifying marks of God's people and gave God's answer: "Lord, who shall abide in thy tabernacle? who shall dwell in thy holy hill? He that walketh uprightly, and worketh righteousness, and speaketh the truth in his heart. He that backbiteth not with his tongue, nor doeth evil to his neighbour, nor taketh up a reproach against his neighbour. In whose eyes a vile person is contemned; but he honoureth them that fear the Lord. He that sweareth to his own hurt, and changeth not" (Psalm 15:1–4). Honesty and the faithful fulfillment of what we have undertaken are fundamental characteristics of those in whom the Spirit of God is producing His fruit.

A Governing Principle

This fruit—faithfulness to God, to the gospel, and to his own word—governs a spiritual man in every area of his life. It governs his stand for God. Like Paul, he is "set for the defence of the gospel" (Philippians 1:17). His desire, perhaps it would be better to say his determination, is "to withstand in the evil day, and having done all, to stand" for God and His truth (Ephesians 6:13).

The fruit of faithfulness also governs a spiritual man's personal relationships. The command of Ephesians 4:25 expresses the purpose of his heart: "Wherefore putting away lying, speak every man truth with his neighbour: for we are members one of another." The fruit of faithful-ness will control his marriage relations, his family relations, his church relations, and even his business relations. No area of a Christian's life is remote from the activity of the Holy Spirit within him. The Spirit who brought him to saving faith will mature him through sanctifying faith with the result that faithfulness to Christ will govern every sphere of his life. As he trusts the Lord, he is made trustworthy, just like his Master.

Meek, but Not Weak

"The fruit of the Spirit is . . . meekness."
Galatians 5:23

To most people meekness is weakness. That is understandable because meekness is a word that usually designates a person who is submissive, non-assertive, mild, sweet, unthreatening, and gentle—altogether a peaceful and passive sort of person. Such a temperament is recognized as good and "nice," but it is usually despised and ridiculed as anemic. In most schools children who appear too passive or submissive will probably be educated to be bolder and more self-assertive. In business, companies usually advertise for "aggressive" people for sales and leadership positions. In other words, in our society meekness is dismissed as weakness.

That perception makes it difficult to relate what the Bible teaches about meekness. Jesus said, "Blessed are the meek, for they shall inherit the earth" (Matthew 5:5). Unconverted people find it difficult to understand why God places such a premium on weakness. The truth is that He does not. In the word of God meekness is not weakness but the strength of faith. It is true that meekness describes a gentle, humble, patient spirit that would prefer to crucify self rather than glorify it. It is true that meekness describes an attitude of inner peace and a capacity to handle the pressures of life—whether they are from provoking people or from adverse circumstances—without malice, bitterness, or anger. But the biblical meaning of the term goes much deeper.

From most of what we have noted thus far, you could be forgiven for mistaking meekness as a mere type of personality. On the contrary, the Bible describes it as the fruit of the Holy Spirit. It is the product of the Holy Spirit's imparting grace in the life of a believer in Christ. Archbishop Trench says, "It is an inwrought grace of the soul, and the expression of it is first and chiefly toward God. It is the temper and spirit in which we accept His dealings with us as good, and therefore without disputing or resisting."

Meekness grows out of faith. That is why I defined it as the strength of faith. The apostle James speaks of "the meekness of wisdom" (James 3:13). Factoring this insight into the definition of the term we may say that meekness is the exercise of faith in God, in His love, and in His wisdom, tempering our response to people and to circumstances.

Only one person was ever truly and fully meek and that was the Lord Jesus Christ. He testified of Himself, "Take my yoke upon you, and learn of me; for I am meek and lowly in heart" (Matthew 11:29). In His triumphal entry into Jerusalem He fulfilled the prophecy of Zechariah, "Tell ye the daughter of Sion, Behold, thy King cometh unto thee, meek, and sitting upon an ass, and a colt the foal of an ass" (Matthew 21:5). The attitude of the Lord Jesus was constantly selfless. At His coming into the world He stated His purpose: "Lo, I come (in the volume of the book it is written of me,) to do thy will, O God" (Hebrews 10:7). In the midst of His earthly ministry He summarized the reason for all He did: "My meat is to do the will of him that sent me, and to finish his work" (John 4:34). In the Garden of Gethsemane as He approached the cross He prayed, "Father, if thou be willing, remove this cup from me: nevertheless not my will, but thine, be done" (Luke 22:42). That is perfect meekness.

With that meekness the Lord Jesus Christ could always look beyond the circumstances, the suffering, and even the human agents of His pain in the assurance that God was accomplishing His will. In this He is the pattern for all His people. "Christ . . . suffered for us, leaving us an example, that ye should follow his steps: who did no sin, neither was guile found in his mouth: who, when he was reviled, reviled not again; when he suffered, he threatened not; but committed himself to him that judgeth righteously" (1 Peter 2:21–23). This does not mean that He was weak or accepting of all the wickedness of men. This is the same Jesus who powerfully castigated the Pharisees in uncompromising terms and who twice stormed into the temple and whipped the traders who were defiling the house of God. There was no weakness in Christ. His meekness was strength, and in us, meekness—far from being weakness—is Christlike strength to accept and do the will of God, especially when we do not understand it, with a single eye to His glory.

We will therefore consider how the Holy Spirit produces this fruit in us and the effects it has on the various aspects of our lives. The Holy Spirit makes believers joyfully submissive to God's will in all circumstances, even when those circumstances run contrary to our personal desires and comfort, thereby enabling us to maintain a sweet, submissive attitude to the Lord, and a gentle, patient spirit toward men, so that we may live with inner peace whatever is happening around us or to us.

The mention of inner peace should make this immediately interesting to us all. It seems that just about everyone is looking for peace and that most are not finding it. Many Christians admit that they are living in a state of turmoil and that the idea of being at peace with themselves and with their circumstances is something that sounds too good to be true. As long as Christians embrace the aggressive, self-assertive attitude of the world they will exclude themselves from enjoying the peace that God has for His people. So it is of the utmost importance to our usefulness to God and to our own peace of heart and mind that we cultivate the fruit of meekness.

How the Holy Spirit Produces Meekness

We may be sure that in producing the fruit of meekness the Holy Spirit will frequently put us in the place where we will have to exercise meekness. There is an old saying that "practice makes perfect." Certainly, in the Lord's army there are plenty of training exercises. We may pinpoint four particular ways of the Spirit's working.

The Spirit Wrestles with Our Flesh

The first way by which the Spirit produces meekness in us is by wrestling with our flesh. Genesis 32:24–31, the record of the Lord's dealing with Jacob at Peniel, gives us a perfect example of how the Lord does this. In this passage He takes a naturally self-centered, vehement, and at times even vicious man and makes him a spiritual prince. When Jacob was left alone, "there wrestled a man with him until the breaking of the day. And when he saw that he prevailed not against him, he touched the hollow of his thigh; and the hollow of Jacob's thigh was out of joint, as he wrestled with him. And he said, Let me go, for the day breaketh. And he said, I will not let thee go, except thou bless me. And he said unto him, What is thy name? And he said, Jacob. And he said, Thy name shall be called no more Jacob, but Israel: for as a prince hast thou power with God and with men, and hast prevailed. And Jacob asked him, and said, Tell me, I pray thee, thy name. And he said, Wherefore is it that thou dost ask after my name? And he blessed him there. And Jacob called the name of the place Peniel: for I have seen God face to face, and my life is preserved. And as he passed over Penuel the sun rose upon him, and he halted upon his thigh" (Genesis 32:24–31).

Let us try to understand the spiritual implications of the story. The Lord was doing great work in Jacob, creating a major character change in him. Such a work could start in only one place, the place of solitary wrestling with God. This was not an easy experience for Jacob for the angel of the Lord did not change him by a word of divine command. No, he wrestled with him. In that wrestling the Lord touched the source of Jacob's fleshly strength and changed him there. This is what is necessary in all of us if we are to become so altered as to produce meekness, the fruit of the Spirit. God must deal with our flesh—with the things in which we imagine ourselves to be strong—and remove all carnal dependence upon self. The force of the flesh is always the chief enemy of the fruit of the Spirit. It is by subduing our flesh that the Spirit produces His fruit in us.

The Spirit Witnesses to Our Faith
The second way in which the Holy Spirit produces the fruit of meekness in us is by witnessing to our faith. Here Job provides a good example. Job was a patient man who became vehement and bitter because he could not understand why God was inflicting almost every kind of suffering on him. His was the problem that sooner or later forces itself on us all. Every pastor has had Christians with burdened hearts come and ask for help in understanding the problem of their pain: "Why does God allow this pain or trouble in my life? I cannot understand why such things are happening to me. God appears to be angry with me and yet I do not know of any particular sin that has caused His anger; otherwise I would deal with it. I love and worship the Lord and He has only to say the word and my affliction will be removed. But He does not say the word. In fact He does not seem to say anything, for I cannot seem to get through to Him, even in prayer. Why is this?" There is no easy, one-answer-fits-all solution to such a

problem. Many, indeed most, suggested answers are demonstrably wrong. That was so in Job's case as his supposedly wise friends made his sufferings worse with their vicious accusation that he must have been guilty of great hidden sin to have landed in such trouble. In many other cases they would probably have been right in reaching such a conclusion, but in Job's case they could not have been more wrong. After all these years, few of us have progressed beyond the folly of Job's "miserable comforters," as he called them. When we are enduring the agony of some deep sorrow or pain, it seems that there will always be some well meaning Christian intent on imposing his wisdom on us, whose only contribution is to join in Satan's attack on us. In times of suffering we need to have the Lord come and minister His word to our hearts.

In Job's peculiar case, it took a long time for that to happen. Job was expected to take his stand on what he already knew of the Lord and to judge his circumstances by what he knew of God—not to judge God by his circumstances. Finally, the Lord appeared to him, but even then Job did not understand the *why* of his sufferings any more than he did at the beginning. What the Lord did, however, was far more important to Job's peace of mind. He revealed His own wisdom, power, and glory, thereby convincing Job of His all-wise, sovereign purpose. Job knew that the Lord knew what He was doing. When he came to that wonderful realization, Job was still suffering all his old pain. Now, however, his eyes were on the Lord, not on his suffering. Through the pain he rejoiced in his sovereign Lord. The faith that the Lord knew what He was doing in allowing him to endure pain and trouble lifted Job from the depths of despair and from the hurtful folly of his friends to the peace of a meek and quiet spirit.

We are all called to "run with patience the race that is set before us" (Hebrews 12:1). Patience is closely related to meekness and it comes from keeping our eyes on the Lord. "Looking unto Jesus," is how Paul puts it (Hebrews 12:2). We all need to have Job's experience of grasping the truth of the all-wise sovereignty of God. We all need to be overwhelmed by His glory and power. When that happens we will not be overwhelmed by life's troubles. We will not become petulant or rebellious against God for allowing such things to happen to us. We will, on the contrary, humbly accept His dealings with us as perfect and say, "Thy will be done in me, as it is in heaven." Thus the Holy Spirit witnesses to our faith to produce in us the fruit of meekness.

The Spirit Whispers to Us in Our Fainting

There is a third way in which the Holy Spirit produces meekness in us: He whispers to us in our fainting. Take the case of Elijah as a beautiful example. Elijah was a mighty man of God, the prophet of fire. A manlier, stronger, more courageous, or more faithful man than Elijah would be difficult to find, even among the heroes of Scripture. He had been God's instrument in performing a great miracle. He had called fire down from heaven, had slain the prophets of Baal, and had prayed down the rain of God's blessing on a drought-ridden land. Here was a man who had done a great work, bravely standing alone to defy the eight hundred fifty false prophets against him. Every one of those apostate prophets was ready to kill him, but he did not flinch. In addition, Ahab the king would gladly have murdered him, but Elijah showed no fear. Then he received what W. P. Nicholson called "a love letter from Jezebel" in which she promised to kill him. Suddenly his heart sank and the man who had stood like a rock against all the forces against him said to himself, "All I have done is in vain. I called down the fire of God, but Jezebel is still there. I prayed down rain from heaven, but Jezebel is still there. I have rid the land of these prophets of Baal, but Jezebel is still there. My life and work are all in vain."

We come to strange conclusions and take inexplicable steps when we are depressed. A sane man could never have reached the conclusion that Elijah's life was in vain, but Elijah was so depressed that he was not thinking sanely at that point. So he ran away and cried, "O Lord, take away my life" (1 Kings 19:4). The Lord's gracious response was to meet with His distraught prophet. The first thing He did was to let him rest. Then He fed him. As Elijah slept under a juniper tree, "behold, then an angel touched him, and said unto him, Arise and eat. And he looked, and, behold, there was a cake baken on the coals, and a cruse of water at his head. And he did eat and drink, and laid him down again. And the angel of the Lord came again the second time, and touched him, and said, Arise and eat; because the journey is too great for thee" (1 Kings 19:7). The next thing the Lord did was to lead Elijah to the mount of God where he spoke to him, not by wind or earthquake or fire, but by a still small voice. As he arrived at the mount, Elijah was still overwrought. He was inclined to be argumentative with the Lord. His words dripped with the anger of disappointed hopes. But the Lord's whisper subdued the prophet's strident outbursts and restored him to the place of submissive service and usefulness.

This is how the Lord deals with His hurting servants: "A bruised reed shall he not break, and smoking flax shall he not quench, till he send forth judgment unto victory" (Matthew 12:20). When we are depressed and fainting, feeling that we have failed God or perhaps even that God has failed us, the Lord could well be angry at our unbelief. He could respond with the voice of thunder or with burning words of fire. Instead, He comforts us with gospel rest, feeds us with the bread of heaven, brings us near to Himself in the mount of communion, and encourages us with a still small voice. He knows how to whisper in the ears of a fainting Elijah. He assures us, "Fear thou not; for I am with thee: be not dismayed; for I am thy God: I will strengthen thee; yea, I will help thee; yea, I will uphold thee with the right hand of my righteousness" (Isaiah 41:10). The soft whisper of grace is often how the Holy Spirit draws us back from bitter resentment at our perceived failure and replaces it with the fruit of meekness.

The Spirit Works with Us in Our Failures

The fourth way in which the Holy Spirit produces meekness in us is by working with us in our failures. We may take the case of Peter as an outstanding illustration. Peter was a good man who loved the Lord Jesus. He was capable of doing great things for God. He was a man of immense zeal and at times of intemperate vehemence, even of boastfulness. He boasted that though all the other disciples should forsake the Lord Jesus, he certainly would not. He would gladly die for Him. Peter meant and felt all this, so much so that he paid no heed to the warning of the Master that he would deny Him. He did deny Christ, asserting with oaths and curses that he did not even know Him. At that point Peter hit rock bottom. He went out and wept bitterly, feeling his cowardice and no doubt convinced that His sinful failure was the final chapter of his biography.

It was not the final chapter. As Winston Churchill said when Britain was at her lowest point in World War II, "This is not the end. It is not the beginning of the end. It is only the end of the beginning." So it was with Peter's failure. Afterwards, the Lord Jesus took great care to restore him. He revealed Himself to Peter soon after His resurrection. He invited Peter particularly to meet him in Galilee, singling him out as one He especially desired to see. When He met with His disciples in Galilee He carefully probed Peter's heart with the thrice repeated question, "Lovest thou me?" (John 21:15–17). Three times the Saviour elicited Peter's honest response, "Thou knowest that I love Thee." Then He commissioned him, "Feed my lambs, feed my sheep." Peter was thus restored.

However, he still needed to grow in meekness. His impetuous spirit still led him into trouble. Having received his own commission from the Lord, he at once inquired regarding John, "Lord, and what will this man do?" (John 21:21). The Lord Jesus had to rebuke his intrusion. "If I will that he tarry till I come, what is that to thee? follow thou me" (John 21:22). This was Christ's great objective in working with Peter. It was to make him a wholly consecrated follower, one who would unquestioningly do His will and serve Him to the end. In Peter's case, this work was entirely successful. By working with him through his failures, the Lord Jesus made Peter a model of meekness and loyalty in His service.

We see much of ourselves when we look into the life of Peter. Our impetuosity often betrays us as Peter's did him. Our baseless self-confidence leads us into failure and backsliding. And when we fail the Lord we naturally imagine that all useful service is at an end. It is not. The Lord Jesus still does not break a bruised reed. He is the great restorer. Our carnal dependence on, and promotion of, self and our arrogant running ahead of the will of God must be brought under subjection to Christ. When from the depths of our failure we confess the sins that brought us there we will find that the Holy Spirit works with us precisely as Jesus did with Peter. He does not give up on His people. He lifts them up—and He does it by putting down their flesh and making them His meek and lowly servants.

The Evidences of Meekness

The fruit of meekness will be evident first in relation to God, second in relation to others, and third in relation to ourselves.

Godward Evidences

The first evidence of meekness is that *we will heartily receive God's word*. We are commanded, "Wherefore lay apart all filthiness and superfluity of naughtiness, and receive with meekness the engrafted word, which is able to save your souls" (James 1:21). The only way a Christian can receive God's word is with meekness. Without meekness we set ourselves up as judges of the word (when instead the word should judge us) and we shut our hearts against what the Lord has to say to us. The inevitable result is much confusion and misery. By contrast, meekness says, "Speak, Lord; for thy servant heareth" (1 Samuel 3:9).

The second Godward evidence of meekness is that *we will embrace His will*. Peter described the meekness of the Lord Jesus Christ: "When he was reviled, [he] reviled not again; when he suffered, he threatened not; but committed himself to him that judgeth righteously" (1 Peter 2:23). That is how meekness works. Under the pressure of adverse circumstances, we would naturally vent our anger and assert our rights. We often become rebellious against the Lord for allowing us to be treated badly by others. A meek spirit, however, recognizes that the Lord does all things well and that he puts us into the situations we face as a testimony to His glory. God's will is always good enough for a man of meekness.

A third Godward evidence of meekness is *that we will walk so as to be worthy of Christ's name*. This is the characteristic walk of a Christian: "Walk worthy of the vocation wherewith ye are called, with all lowliness and meekness, with longsuffering, forbearing one another in love" (Ephesians 4:1–2). Lowliness and meekness—not the flashy talents that the world associates with success—make our lives worthy of our Saviour's name. If we are meek we will fulfil God's purpose for us: "Put on therefore, as the elect of God, holy and beloved, bowels of mercies, kindness, humbleness of mind, meekness, longsuffering" (Colossians 3:12). In every situation the questions we must answer are, What can I do in this situation to glorify God? What would be worthy of His name? The question is never, What will gratify or satisfy me? If we are responding to some evil that others have done to us, we are not to ask, How may I vindicate myself or revenge myself? Rather, we must ask, What is the course of action that will glorify God? This is God's purpose for us. Meekness keeps us aware of this fact. It never allows us to forget that the name of the Lord is involved in all we do. It will endure anything to magnify that name and will never willingly act so as to bring dishonor on it.

Manward Evidences

People can be very difficult to deal with. They pose the most constant challenge to our being meek. When others are mean to us we naturally feel that we should give as good as we get. Paul instructs us in such situations "to speak evil of no man, to be no brawlers, but gentle, shewing all meekness unto all men" (Titus 3:2). As Christians we are called upon to do right, even when we are dealing with those who have done us wrong. Our old man would urge us to act in a carnal, threatening, or vengeful way, but the Spirit of God urges us to be meek and to expect God to bless our meekness for His own glory.

By showing meekness to all men we will be patient when we are provoked by trying people. We will remember that we have more than an argument to win. We aim to win souls. Therefore we will do as Paul advised and "in meekness [instruct] those that oppose themselves; if God peradventure will give them repentance to the acknowledging of the truth" (2 Timothy 2:25).

Meekness toward others will mean that we will be humbly conscious of our own weakness and will be ready to restore a fallen brother in love. This is precisely what Paul admonished the Galatians to do, and it is significant that his command comes immediately after his treatment of the fruit of the Spirit: "Brethren, if a man be overtaken in a fault, ye which are spiritual, restore such an one in the spirit of meekness; considering thyself, lest thou also be tempted" (Galatians 6:1). We have a saying when we witness the fall or calamity of others: "There, but for the grace of God, go I." It is meekness that honestly makes such a confession and stirs our love to reach out to lift up the fallen.

This spirit of meekness enables us to bear powerful witness to the ungodly of the great hope that Christ has placed in our hearts. If we meekly face circumstances that drive Christless souls to distraction, we give a powerful witness to saints and sinners, but especially to sinners. Peter said, "Sanctify the Lord God in your hearts: and be ready always to give an answer to every man that asketh you a reason of the hope that is in you with meekness and fear" (1 Peter 3:15). Unsaved people want to see the effects of God's saving grace in our lives. They want to see evidence that it works! Meekness demonstrates that it does.

Inward Evidences

Our experience of this fruit of meekness, just as of any other Christian virtue, is imperfect while we are in this world, but it will be real. Its evidences in our lives will be powerful and plentiful. With this grace, we will live with inward peace whatever our outward circumstances. That is a glorious thing. A meek and quiet spirit enables us to testify with Paul, "I have learned, in whatsoever state I am, therewith to be content. I know both how to be abased, and I know how to abound: every where and in all things I am instructed both to be full and to be hungry, both to abound and to suffer need" (Philippians 4:11–12). This was not an attitude that came naturally to a man of Paul's temperament, for he was the most assertive and passionate of men. But he had found contentment and nothing could destroy it, neither poverty nor pain, neither opposition nor suffering. He testified, "We are troubled on every side, yet not distressed; we are perplexed, but not in despair; persecuted, but not forsaken; cast down, but not destroyed; . . . But though our outward man perish, yet the inward man is renewed day by day. For our light affliction, which is but for a moment, worketh for us a far more exceeding and eternal weight of glory; while we look not at the things which are seen, but at the things which are not seen: for the things which are seen are temporal; but the things which are not seen are eternal. (2 Corinthians 4:8–9, 16–18).

Meekness enables us to live in the enjoyment of God's blessing. Jesus said, "Blessed are the meek" (Matthew 5:5). The world does not believe that for a minute. According to the world if you are meek you are a weak fool, a doormat that people thoughtlessly trample. On the contrary, says the Lord Jesus, the meek will enjoy God's blessing. This is to be expected, for when we live in God's will, receive God's word, and walk worthy of His name, we will assuredly have God's blessing upon us.

Most of all, meekness will make us more like Christ. To be like Christ is the desire that underpins all a Christian is and does. Paul wrote, "I . . . beseech you by the meekness and gentleness of Christ" (2 Corinthians 10:1). Peter wrote, "As Christ hath suffered for us in the flesh, arm yourselves likewise with the same mind: for he that hath suffered in the flesh hath ceased from sin" (1 Peter 4:1). Without attempting an exposition of this verse let us note a clear moral implication in it: If we endure suffering with the mind of Christ, we will not fall into sin on account of our suffering, but will be more sanctified and made more like Christ by means of it. We are never more like Christ than when we bow and say, "Father, not my will but thine, be done." This is true meekness, the fruit of the Spirit.

Having Command of Ourselves

"The fruit of the Spirit is . . . temperance."
Galatians 5:23

We have already noted that the nine virtues listed in Galatians 5:22–23 fall into three groups of three and that in each group the first mentioned virtue governs the other two. Thus faith is the governing idea in the last group. Faith teaches us that trust in Christ makes us trustworthy. Meekness teaches us that trust in Christ leads us to accept God's dealings with us as good. Temperance teaches us that trust in Christ enables us to control and restrain the natural expressions of self and sin.

The Greek word *enkrateia*, "temperance," is a combination of two words meaning literally "in strength" or "in power." The idea is of our having inner strength, the power to overcome the impediments of the flesh to our service to God. The word is usually interpreted "self-control," "self-rule," or "moderation." Today, of course, *temperance* describes an attitude to alcoholic drink. The New Testament word goes much further than our use of the modern term, but it does include a proper attitude to alcohol. Albert Barnes, a nineteenth-century American Presbyterian scholar said in his Bible commentary:

> Abstinence from intoxicating drink, as well as from all improper excitement, is demanded by the genius of [the Christian] religion, and on this subject there is no danger of drawing the cords too close. No man was ever injured by the strictest temperance, by total abstinence from ardent spirits, and from wine as a beverage; no man is certainly

safe who does not abstain; no man, it is believed, can be in a proper frame of mind for religious duties who indulges in the habitual use of intoxicating drinks. Nothing does more scandal to religion than such indulgences; and, other things being equal, he is the most under the influence of the Spirit of God who is most thoroughly a man of temperance. (Emphasis added)

It is often claimed that the Bible never commands abstinence from alcohol. The claim is false, for in places the Bible clearly commands abstinence. "Look not thou upon the wine when it is red, when it giveth his colour in the cup, when it moveth itself aright. At the last it biteth like a serpent, and stingeth like an adder" (Proverbs 23:31–32). That the reference here is to fermented wine (we should never forget that the word *wine* in itself does not necessarily indicate an alcoholic beverage), and the command is unmistakably clear. The German commentator Franz Delitzsch says that this verse "warns against the attraction which the wine presents to the sight and to the sense of taste: one must not permit himself to be caught as a prisoner by this enticement, but must maintain his freedom against it." The Scripture leaves no doubt as to how to maintain this freedom: "look not on it." If that is not a command to abstinence, words mean nothing. The appeal of alcoholic wine to the senses of sight and taste is subtle and strong. It is also dangerous, as verse 32 declares, and as Proverbs 20:1 states even more strongly: "Wine is a mocker, strong drink is raging: and whosoever is deceived thereby is not wise." In the face of such danger the command of Scripture is to not even look on alcoholic wine.

Doubtless, some will at once recite verses that appear to contradict this position, but God's word does not contradict itself. If the Bible in one place says that wine is good and acceptable and in another that wine is to be entirely avoided because it is dangerous, surely it is obvious that it is not speaking of the same beverage in both places. Wine that is non-alcoholic is good; wine that is alcoholic is not. When we remember that in Bible times alcoholic wine was weak by present-day standards (the ancients had not discovered how to fortify wines or to distill spirits), the command to abstain is all the more noteworthy. If we are commanded to not even look on a weak alcoholic wine, what shall we say of those who claim the right to imbibe not only fortified wine but strong liquors? Such people tell us that the Bible allows the consumption of alcohol, but not in excess; it is too much alcohol that is hurtful, not the moderate consumption of it. However, Solomon did not merely say that we must shun over-consumption. What he said was that we should shun the very sight and taste of alcoholic wine. Too much of anything is hurtful. Too much water is fatal! So it is not only the *misuse* of alcohol, but the *use* of it that Proverbs 23:31 prohibits.

Abstinence from alcohol is one form of self-restraint, but when Paul says that the fruit of the Spirit is temperance he means something more radical. Temperance is the opposite of the driving force behind "the works of the flesh" (Galatians 5:19–21). What lies behind the works of the flesh is self-indulgence. Temperance is the opposite of self-indulgence. It is total abstinence from all things forbidden—no matter how the flesh craves them—and the avoidance of excess in satisfying all permissible desires. A Christian is not to be governed by his own desires, or his own impulses, but by the Holy Spirit. John Brown, the well known Scottish commentator, said that the word means "self command and denotes the right attitude of mind, heart, and life, in reference to those objects in the world which naturally call forth our desires, whether it be pleasure, profit, or reputation." Thus temperance means that we deny the right of the flesh to dominate us and that we so regulate our lives that Christ, His kingdom, and His glory are the determining factors in all that we purpose and in all that we do. Paul wrote, "If ye then be risen with Christ, seek those things which are above, where Christ sitteth on the right hand of God. Set your affection on things above, not on things on the earth. For ye are dead, and your life is hid with Christ in God. . . . Mortify therefore your members which are upon the earth; fornication, uncleanness, inordinate affection, evil concupiscence, and covetousness, which is idolatry" (Colossians 3:1–3, 5). In a similar vein he told the Galatians: "They that are Christ's have crucified the flesh with the affections and lusts" (Galatians 5:24). Crucifying the flesh with the affections and lusts—that is temperance. Thus this aspect of the fruit of the Spirit treats temperance as the victory of the Spirit over the flesh.

Not Sinless Perfection

The fruit of the Spirit is not sinless perfection. Some preachers give the impression that sinless perfection is not only desirable—every Christian desires perfect holiness—but attainable here and now. Some go so far as to teach that a Christian may make a decision of commitment and by that act of faith be perfectly sanctified instantaneously. Many who profess that sort of theology testify to a two-stage work of grace. They will give the date of their conversion to Christ and another date, perhaps months or years later, when they had the root of sin burned out and they became sinlessly perfect. From that moment they became like corpses, so thoroughly dead to sin as not to react to any stimulus of the world, the flesh, or the devil. There are other theories of the perfectionism. Some perfectionists ask, "Can God keep us from sinning for one tenth of a second? Can He do it for a second? If He can keep us sinless for one second, can He do it for one minute? If He can do it for one minute, what about His doing it for one hour, or one day, or one week, or one month, or one year? Can He not therefore keep us from sinning for the rest of our lives?" The implication is that God is willing to make us sinlessly perfect at once and we have no reason to be less than sinless. All the questions are based on a false foundation. Their premise is an error that betrays a totally unscriptural view of what constitutes sin.

Paul disposes with every claim of perfectionism with his words to the Romans and to the Galatians: "In me (that is, in my flesh,) dwelleth no good thing" (Romans 7:18). And in our text, he calls for self-restraint or self-control, a term that has no meaning to people who have had the old man burned out of them. There would be no need for self-restraint if we felt the attractions of sin no more than a corpse feels sensation. Self-restraint, or self-rule implies fighting and subduing the natural propensities of the flesh. Paul fully describes this conflict in Romans 7. That chapter does not describe an unsaved man or a carnal Christian, but the experience of the great apostle himself. This man, who loved and served the Lord with such eminent success, who walked in victorious holiness, confessed that his old man—which is never reconstructed, but remains what it is, the old man, with all its hatred of God and godliness—is in constant opposition to the work of grace in his soul. "To will is present with me; but how to perform that which is good I find not. For the good that I would I do not: but the evil which I would not, that I do. . . . I find then a law, that, when I would do good, evil is present with me. For I delight in the law of God after the inward man: but I see another law in my members, warring against the law of my mind, and bringing me into captivity to the law of sin which is in my members" (Romans 7:18–19, 21–23). In the light of this very real spiritual conflict, Paul's cry was no empty rhetorical flourish: "O wretched man that I am! who shall deliver me from the body of this death?" (Romans 7:24). "Who shall deliver me?" Paul knew the answer to that question and rejoiced, "I thank God through Jesus Christ our Lord" (verse 25). But that victory was just that, a subduing of an enemy, an overcoming of a strong opponent. For Paul the fruit of the Spirit was not exemption from battling the lusts of the flesh but the power to "keep under [or, discipline] my body, and bring it into subjection" (1 Corinthians 9:27). The fruit of the Spirit is not sinless perfection; it is the subduing of the flesh, not its elimination.

A Fruit, Not a Work

Gaining control of ourselves is not a work of self but a fruit of God's Holy Spirit. It is not a matter of will power or of making resolutions. This needs to be emphasized against all the pressure that preachers are wont to impose on people to settle their problems with the flesh by making a (preferably public) decision or commitment. Doubtless there are times when Christians have sinned against God and need to make confession and seek forgiveness. However, when they have done so they will still need to carry on an unremitting warfare against the flesh. One decision, one trip down a church aisle, will not produce this fruit of self-rule. It is altogether tragic that in most Bible-believing churches sincere believers are being misled and frustrated by the notion that if they will only make the right decision they will be freed from the old man's virulent opposition to all things spiritual. Many well meaning Christians have tried to act on such theories and have found to their horror that after all their "good decisions" in response to preachers' appeals they are nothing bettered. The subjection of the flesh is not achieved by any work of ours.

Nor is self-rule the product of natural ability. It is not produced by our education or our culture. High standards of education and culture may make certain expressions of fleshly lust undesirable. For example, in certain cultures drunkenness is despicable and such cultures are therefore helps to sobriety. However, while they make certain expressions of fleshly lust unacceptable and undesirable, they will leave us with others just as vicious. The simple fact is that the flesh cannot deny the flesh. The flesh cannot crucify itself. This is a spiritual matter. The Holy Spirit produces the subduing of the flesh as a spiritual fruit, the harvest of grace in the soul of the believer. That harvest is a reaping of the benefits of the work of Christ on our behalf. Grace provides the seed in the gospel, grace plants that seed in us in the new birth, and grace nourishes the seed in sanctification as the Holy Spirit blesses the means of grace, especially the word and prayer, to our souls. Peter indicates how Christians enter into the experience of this abundant harvest of grace: "Add to your faith virtue; and to virtue knowledge; and to knowledge temperance; and to temperance patience; and to patience godliness; and to godliness brotherly kindness; and to brotherly kindness charity" (2 Peter 1:5–7). *Add* means "supply" or "bring together in proper combination and correspondence" (John Brown). With this meaning of the word in mind, we follow the steps set out by Peter, at least as far as his mention of self-control: By your faith supply virtue—that is, moral goodness or energy; and by your virtue supply knowledge—that is, exercise zeal for substantial scriptural knowledge; make sure that all your moral energy is directed by knowledge, so that it does not degenerate into misdirected zeal; and by your knowledge supply self-control—that is, self-control is a virtue that arises out of genuine spiritual knowledge, namely, the knowledge of Christ revealed in Scripture and apprehended by our faith. This is how a goodly crop of self-control will spring up in a believer's life. It is a fruit to be cultivated, not a work of the flesh.

The Basis of Self-Control

Self-control depends on a true grasp of grace as to its sources, channels, and experience. Only by knowing the gospel will we bear the fruit of the Spirit. Many define the gospel as a message that shows people how to escape hell and get to heaven. They hold that once a person has received Christ as Saviour, the gospel recedes into the background, at least as far as having any vital part in living the Christian life is concerned. They will insist that salvation is by grace through faith, but they present the Christian life as the practice of various sets of what they deem to be moral or spiritual principles. This is a species of legalism, for it is living by rules or laws. Sanctification is viewed as obedience to a set of external standards, compliance with rules or "spiritual principles." But according to the New Testament *we live by faith, not by rule.* Godly living will observe God's law, but its source of power is grace received through faith in Christ. In other words, the gospel is the basis of all godly living. We must grasp the gospel and particularly the truth of our justification by the imputation of Christ's righteousness and the truth of our acceptance by virtue of our union with Christ our righteousness. It is only as we do so that we will have the power necessary to realize our sanctification. Peter plainly teaches this truth. Note especially the portions emphasized in the following passage: "Simon Peter, a servant and an apostle of Jesus Christ, to them that have obtained like precious faith with us *through the right-eousness of God and our Saviour Jesus Christ:* Grace and peace be multiplied unto you *through the knowledge of God, and of Jesus our Lord,* according as his divine power hath given unto us all things that pertain unto life and godliness, *through the knowledge of him that hath called us to glory and virtue*" (2 Peter 1:1–3). Peter later returned to this theme of the power of knowing Christ as revealed in the gospel: "Grow in grace, and in the knowledge of our Lord and Saviour Jesus Christ" (2 Peter 3:18).

As He equips us to bring forth the fruit of self-control the Holy Spirit always leads us into a deeper grasp of the gospel. The more we see of Christ, the more we will understand our freedom from guilt, condemnation, and bondage, and the more we will be able to love and trust Him. This is what provides the foundation for a life that is truly temperate or moderate, under control.

Submission to the Spirit the Key

Submission to the Spirit's control is therefore the key to self-control. Tem-perance is the fruit of the Spirit. We can enjoy this fruit only as we "walk in the Spirit." There is a clear connection between "walk in the Spirit" (Galatians 5:16) and "the fruit of the Spirit" (Galatians 5:22). To walk in the Spirit is to live under His control. It is submission to the leadership and the lordship of the Holy Spirit: "Be not drunk with wine, wherein is excess; but be filled with the Spirit" (Ephesians 5:18). "Be constantly full" or live under the control of the Holy Spirit. When a police officer pulls over a drunk driver he charges him with "driving under the influence." Christians are not to be under the influence of alcohol, but they are to live under the controlling influence of the Spirit.

To be governed by the Spirit is to be governed by His word. We may restate that truth like this: It is only as a Christian ignores or disobeys what the Holy Spirit says in His word that he can fail to produce the fruit of the Spirit. In other words, this fruit of the Spirit is attainable by all Christians. This is not a standard of Christian living for a small elite; it is for us all. We are alive in Christ, united to Him, and the Holy Spirit constantly applies the merits of Christ by means of His word. If we take time with the Bible and pray over it, and obey it, we will be submitting ourselves to the controlling influence of the Holy Spirit. He will lead us through love, joy, peace, longsuffering, gentleness, goodness, faith, and meekness to the experience of temperance. Controlling us and enabling us to govern the lusts and appetites of the flesh, He will lead us to live for the glory of the Lord Jesus Christ. He will fix our eyes on things that are unseen and eternal (2 Corinthians 4:18). This is the essence of the virtue of temperance. "He that hath an ear, let him hear what the Spirit saith unto the churches" (Revelation 2:7).

Genuine Christian Liberty

"Against such there is no law."
Galatians 5:24

After Paul lists the virtues that constitute the fruit of the Spirit, he says, "Against such there is no law." Unfortunately, preachers pass rather lightly over this little statement. It is as if Paul's way of ending his treatment of the fruit of the Spirit were somehow inconsequential, a rhetorical device that adds little to the passage. Yet Paul was inspired to include this text for a good reason. In the context of the argument of the epistle in general, the statement "against such there is no law" is significant. In the context of the argument of chapter 5 in particular, it is necessary to complete the thought that the apostle has carefully developed.

The subject of Galatians 5 is life in the liberty of the Spirit contrasted with life in the bondage of the law and of the flesh. Paul's contention is that the Judaizers then seeking to influence the new Galatian Christians were ignoring the distinction between the moral and the ceremonial law of God. The moral law is universal and enduring. The ceremonial law was Jewish and temporary. Failing to mark this distinction, the Judaizers who were attacking the Galatian churches were making the law an instrument of bondage. The crux of Paul's argument against this attack is that to a Christian the law is not the enemy of life in the Spirit or of the true liberty of the gospel. Having expounded the theme of life in the fullness of the fruit of the Spirit, the apostle says, "Against such there is no law."

Our subject therefore is life in the Spirit in relation to God's law. It could be argued that this is not merely the subject of this text but of the New Testament generally. Anyone who does not come to grips with this subject has not laid hold of the true meaning and application of the gospel of Jesus Christ. Dealing with the subject of the fruit of the Spirit in relation to God's law, Paul makes the point that the law is not against the fruit of the Spirit, and the fruit of the Spirit is not against the law.

The Law Is Not Contrary to Life in the Spirit

The first and most obvious truth laid down in our text is that there is nothing in God's law that is contrary to life in the Spirit. It will help if we remember the background to Paul's statement. Controversy was wrecking the Galatian churches. Certain Judaizers were trying to impose the entire Old Testament legal system on these new Gentile believers. The Judaizers did not deny the deity of Christ, the efficacy of His blood, or His resurrection from the dead. They did not even deny justification by faith. What they denied was justification by faith *alone*. Particularly, they denied that anyone, even a Gentile, could be a Christian without also being a Jew. That meant attaching the entire system of Judaism to the gospel. When Paul refused to do this, the Judaizers charged him with despising and dishonoring the law. According to them, the law of God was the enemy of Paul's theology and vice versa. Paul argued that he was innocent of the charge and that the Judaizers were guilty of betraying both the law and the gospel. Follow his argument:

The gospel is the gospel of liberty (Galatians 5:1–3). Liberty from what? Liberty from the bondage of seeking justification by law keeping. Christian liberty is the liberty from having to establish our acceptance with God by the merits of our own works. Assured of full acceptance on the ground of Christ's imputed righteousness, believers are free to serve God, not to gain His favor but because they have received it as a gift. Ultimately, Christian liberty is the freedom of a believer to experience the love of God and to express his love for God by a life that pleases Him.

Thus, *Christian liberty is not license to sin but freedom from sin's dominion so that one can live a life of holiness by faith in Jesus Christ.* Paul warns against turning liberty into license: "Brethren, ye have been called unto liberty; only use not liberty for an occasion to the flesh, but by love

serve one another" (Galatians 5:13). Today it is all too common for professing Christians to define Christian liberty as liberty to live like the
world. To many Christians, liberty denotes their "right" to use tobacco
or to drink alcohol. When asked why then they oppose the smoking of
marijuana these "liberated Christians" usually reply that it is illegal.
When the state legalizes the use of marijuana—as has happened in various places already—such people will have no real reason to oppose it.
It is not far-fetched to imagine professing Christians proudly proclaim-
ing their liberty to smoke pot. After all, they already indulge in the use
of the powerful killer drugs of their choice and excuse themselves that
they have the liberty in Christ to do so. What a travesty of Paul's
teaching! Christian liberty is not a cloak for worldliness. It is the liberty
to be holy, to be like Christ. The Christian's liberty is freedom to live
on "higher ground" by faith in Christ, not to make that faith the excuse
to continue in fleshly lusts.

*The Holy Spirit leads His people to exercise their liberty by constantly
warring against the flesh.* "This I say then, Walk in the Spirit, and ye
shall not fulfil the lust of the flesh. For the flesh lusteth against the
Spirit, and the Spirit against the flesh: and these are contrary the one to
the other: so that ye cannot do the things that ye would" (Galatians
5:16–17). Only those who have received the Spirit in regeneration have
the ability to battle against the flesh, not merely against some particular aspects of its lusting. Without the Holy Spirit, men will always
entrench the power of the flesh, even when they appear to be opposing
some particular lust. Thus their "righteousnesses," as the Bible calls
men's efforts at being good, "are as filthy rags" (Isaiah 64:6), because
they fortify the rebellion of the flesh against God even as they appear
to fight its excesses. In contrast, the Holy Spirit leads His people to
fight the flesh, not just a few of its worst features. Holiness is not the
curbing of the most obvious outbursts of fleshly lust; it is the conquest
of the principle of the flesh as well as of its power. Christian liberty is
the freedom to be active and successful in this battle.

Life in the Spirit is not only a life of fighting but of fruitfulness. "The
fruit of the Spirit is love, joy, peace, longsuffering, gentleness, goodness, faith, meekness, temperance" (Galatians 5:22–23), and the law is
not against these things. The Holy Spirit leads Christians to produce
such fruit. In other words, He leads them to live in the love of Christ,
in the joy of sins forgiven, in the peace of their acceptance with God,
and in the blessed experience of the results of these virtues in every

aspect of their lives. There is nothing at all in God's law that is against these virtues. What the law is against is "the works of the flesh"— "adultery, fornication, uncleanness, lasciviousness, idolatry, witchcraft, hatred, variance, emulations, wrath, strife, seditions, heresies, envyings, murders, drunkenness, revellings, and such like: of the which I tell you before, as I have also told you in time past, that they which do such things shall not inherit the kingdom of God" (Galatians 5:19–21). God denounces these works wherever they appear, in a professing Christian as certainly as in an unbeliever. Whatever the flesh produces God's law condemns. It would be easy to multiply proofs of that. "The law is not made for a righteous man, but for the lawless and disobedient, for the ungodly and for sinners, for unholy and profane, for murderers of fathers and murderers of mothers, for manslayers, for whoremongers, for them that defile themselves with mankind, for menstealers, for liars, for perjured persons, and if there be any other thing that is contrary to sound doctrine; according to the glorious gospel of the blessed God, which was committed to my trust" (1 Timothy 1:9–11). The law is not given to condemn a righteous man. It is not the enemy of the fruit of the Spirit but of all that opposes the truth of the glorious gospel. It is against the flesh, as each of the Ten Commandments makes clear. But where in the entire Bible does the law of God condemn any virtue listed under the fruit of the Spirit? The answer is unambiguous: nowhere.

This is a glorious truth upon which Christians should constantly dwell: *God's moral law does not condemn believers in Christ.* Anyone who uses the law to bring a believer in Jesus Christ back under condemnation abuses the law and betrays both the law and the gospel. "There is therefore now no condemnation to them which are in Christ Jesus" (Romans 8:1). Believers in Christ are justified by faith in Him, *legally* justified. God has not broken the law in justifying them; He has fulfilled it. The law condemns all who use it as a means of working their own way to heaven, but it never condemns those who trust in Christ's work to bring them to heaven.

The great point that Paul makes is that believers in Christ are acceptable to the law of God. Every well instructed Christian should know that, but here is an added truth that many do not grasp: The same is true of a Christian's works of faith as is true of himself. The work of faith in a Christian is the fruit of the Spirit. No Christian perfectly exemplifies any of the virtues that constitute the fruit of the

Spirit. We are still works under construction. But here is the glorious truth of justifying grace: The Christian's work is just as truly covered by the merit of Christ as the Christian himself is. This is how God can rejoice in and accept the works of a believer. This is how we can pray and be answered, even though we do not pray perfectly. This is the truth that John lays down in Revelation 8:3, where he tells us that "much incense" is offered with "the prayers of all saints." The same principle applies to all our service for Christ, even though we lament the imperfection that mars it. God accepts it and rejoices in it. Instead of condemning us for our imperfection, He clothes our work of faith in the merit of our Saviour and that makes it acceptable. We do not increase our justification or acceptance by our post-conversion works. Contrary to the dogma of the Church of Rome, justification admits of no degrees; all believers are equally justified. Our works are done in the light of the acceptance that we have in the Lord Jesus Christ. That is a glorious and liberating truth. The moral law does not condemn Christians or the fruit that the Holy Spirit produces in them.

Even the ceremonial law does not condemn life in the Spirit. The ceremonial law prefigured the work of Christ for us and the work of Christ in us. Thus it finds its meaning not in being imposed on Christians but in the Holy Spirit's application to them of all that Christ did on their behalf. Isn't that the essential message of the book of Hebrews? Take for example this statement: "The law having a shadow of good things to come, and not the very image [that is, 'the essential or substantial form'] of the things, can never with those sacrifices which they offered year by year continually make the comers thereunto perfect" (Hebrews 10:1). The chapter goes on to argue that in the Old Testament itself God made it clear that He intended the shadows to endure only for a time. They pointed forward to a glorious fulfillment. Thus, "it is not possible that the blood of bulls and of goats should take away sins" (verse 4). Even the Jews and the most rabid Judaizers who afflicted the early Christian churches had to admit that the actual blood of a bull or a goat could not take away sin. In and of itself animal blood is absolutely valueless as far as moral cleansing is concerned. Its sole function was to point forward to a day when God would send one who would fulfill all the types and shadows. Thus we read, "He taketh away the first [that is, the ceremonial shadow], that he may establish the second [that is, the gospel substance]" (verse 9). So the ceremonial law, far from being against the spiritual fruit of the gospel, was actually a shining light pointing forward to it. The Judaizers perverted even the ceremonial law when they sought to make it permanently binding on believers, even after it had been fulfilled in Christ. Believers should live their life in the realities of the gospel and not in the shadowy figures of the types and pictures of the Old Testament. That is the proper understanding of the law as much as of the gospel, for there is nothing in the moral or ceremonial law that is against life in the Spirit.

Life in the Spirit Is Not Contrary to the Law

The converse of the statement "Against such there is no law" is also true: There is nothing in the life of the Spirit that is contrary to God's law. Paul teaches that there is no controversy between the Spirit and the law. He has already made this point in verses 16–17: "This I say then, Walk in the Spirit, and ye shall not fulfil the lust of the flesh. For the flesh lusteth against the Spirit, and the Spirit against the flesh: and these are contrary the one to the other: so that ye cannot do the things that ye would." Mark the force of this assertion in the light of the statement of our text. In all His work to produce spiritual fruit in us, the Holy Spirit is against the flesh, but He is never against the law of God. There is nothing in the life of the Spirit that is contrary to God's law.

What is the fruit of the Spirit? Surely it is the spiritual fulfillment of our duties to God and to man as set forth in God's law. Indeed, a spiritual application of the precepts of the law is much more penetrating than any legalistic observance of them. While Christians are "led of the Spirit" and are therefore no longer "under the law" (Galatians 5:18), they honor the law by their spiritual obedience to it.

Some Christians appear to think the opposite is true—that to be led by the Spirit means to have no duty to fulfill the precepts of the law. They turn Christianity into Antinomianism. To them, to be "not under law, but under grace" (Romans 6:14) is to be free from the law's strict requirement of holiness. They admit that in Old Testament times God had strict standards of holiness for His people, but they imagine that He has dispensed with such adherence. They persuade themselves that the Spirit allows them to transgress the law of God without displeasing God. There are even Christians who claim the Holy Spirit's direct leading to break God's law! We are inundated by a false spirituality that can justify the most unbiblical behavior with the claim, "I feel that this is what God is leading me to do." For good measure, most of these people condemn as legalists all who want to maintain the standards of the moral law! Against all such self-serving nonsense let us grasp this simple truth: *The Holy Spirit never leads a Christian contrary to His moral law.* According to our text there is nothing illegal in the fruit of the Spirit. What the Spirit produces is never contrary to His law. This is true not only of the nine virtues that constitute the fruit of the Spirit but of all that the Spirit leads us to do. Paul does not say, "Against these things there is no law." No, he says, "Against *such* things there is no law." In other words, these virtues are representative of all that the Holy Spirit leads us to do. Whatever the Spirit produces in us cannot contradict His law. To claim His leading for something that His law condemns is blasphemous.

Grace heightens our observance of God's law and makes it a matter of spiritual joy and liberty. That is one reason the divine definition of regeneration is that the Lord puts His law in the hearts of His people (Hebrews 10:16). As C. H. Spurgeon commented on the statement, "The law of his God is in his heart" (Psalm 37:31), "In the head it puzzles, on the back it burdens, but in the heart it delights." For a Christian, obedience to God's revealed standards is a matter of spiritual joy and liberty, not a matter of bondage.

Christian Obedience to the Law Arises from Gospel Liberty

Having established that there is nothing in God's law that is contrary to the fruit of the Spirit and that there is nothing in the life of the Spirit that is contrary to God's law, we must make one final point: Christians must always be careful to look at obedience to the law from the vantage point of the liberty of the gospel and never the other way around. That is, we obey because we are free and are accepted freely by the Lord. We must never return to the ground of legal obedience in order to gain acceptance with God. Liberty comes by faith in Christ and it is evidenced by victorious obedience. Here is a statement we should never forget. It is the key to much of the Christian life, the answer to the misery and bondage that so many Christians experience: Faith is never the result, but always the cause, of spiritual obedience. "Whatsoever is not of faith is sin" (Romans 14:23). Obedience never produces faith; faith always produces obedience. It cannot exist without the works that prove its existence and reality: "Faith, if it hath not works, is dead, being alone. Yea, a man may say, Thou hast faith, and I have works: shew me thy faith without thy works, and I will shew thee my faith by my works" (James 2:17–18).

This is a vital lesson for God's people to learn if they would live in the joy of spiritual victory. Most of us have grown up believing that, as the little chorus puts it, "obedience is the very best way." In its place this is very true, but out of its proper place it leads to bondage. Preachers call incessantly for obedience, often without saying anything to fortify the faith of their hearers and often without much reference to the truth of the gospel. Obey, obey, obey is the call, as if obedience were possible by the mere determination of the flesh. The power to obey comes solely by faith in Christ. It does not come only because we have come to faith in Christ but by the daily, moment-by-moment exercise of faith in Him.

Every Christian knows how he ought to live. Admittedly, there are some decisions that need special guidance and that therefore call for much pondering and much prayer. However, for the most part, we know what our duty is. What hinders our doing it? The flesh is our chief problem and the only way to overcome the flesh is by faith in Christ crucified: "I am [have been] crucified with Christ: nevertheless I live; yet not I, but Christ liveth in me: and the life which I now live in the flesh I live by the faith of the Son of God, who loved me, and gave himself for me" (Galatians 2:20). That is how we must live. Faith produces obedience. With a clear sight of Christ before him a Christian knows he can do anything the Lord asks of him. Hebrew 11 shows us that those who suffered and died for the cause of God did so by faith, not because they were supermen. They obeyed, even unto death, because they believed. This is liberty, this is joy.

By contrast, those who, by adopting high, scriptural standards, try to achieve a happy, victorious Christian experience succeed only in condemning themselves to endless bondage. There is no liberty to be had in putting our works in the place that Christ should occupy. Christ is the key to vital Christian living and Christ is experienced by a faith that produces obedience, not by an obedience that produces faith. We must always look at this matter of obeying God from the vantage point of the gospel and of our acceptance in Christ. We must never seek to achieve gospel liberty by legal obedience.

From all we have considered in this study, it should be clear that the little clause at the end of Galatians 5:23 forms an important conclusion to Paul's teaching about life in the Spirit:

• The law does not condemn Christian living.

- Christian living honors the law of God, because the Holy Spirit is the author of both.

- Thus faith in Christ is the all-important thing: "In Jesus Christ neither circumcision availeth any thing, nor uncircumcision; but faith which worketh by love" (Galatians 5:6). Here is the key to true Christian liberty, a genuine release from bondage. Here is the secret of power to live as God intends His people to live. Here indeed is the sure way of living with Christian confidence, waiting by faith through the Spirit for the hope of righteousness (Galatians 5:5), so that we will not be ashamed before Christ at His coming (1 John 2:28).

This is liberty indeed.